Acknowledgements

The editors would like to thank the following for their involvement in One Thing I Know:

All contributors and artists for their time, talent and experience.

The European Regional Development Fund and the Creative Industries iNet innovation programme.

Creative England and especially the support of Caroline Norbury and John Newbigin.

Fiasco Design for the layout, book and web design.

These stories have all been taken from the website **www.OneThingIKnow.co.uk**, where you can find an ever expanding store of candid articles.

Book design & layout by Fiasco Design

Cover design by Fiasco Design
Cover illustrations by Little Whale Studio

Printed by EPC Direct Ltd

Foreword

Caroline Norbury
CEO
Creative England

England's creative businesses are already a big success. They generate jobs, profile and value, and they drive innovation. Creative England's objective is to help them raise that ambition further and support them to grow. In particular, we want to address the damaging inequality of access between London and the rest of the country so that talent is not wasted and opportunities are maximised.

Creative England provides practical support so that the best, the brightest and those individuals and companies with the potential to succeed can flourish. Our focus is two-fold. Firstly, to lobby, advocate and champion creative talent and, secondly, to support and help this talent grow through practical and targeted support. This can be via investment, a soft loan, a mentoring programme or by simply putting people in touch with others who can help.

Often, however, it's the small things that are the most important. Our hope is that this collection of personal essays, comments and experiences from the perspective of a wide range of creative entrepreneurs will help you discover your own Eureka moment.

Anthony Story
Editor

There's one request which stands out from working with a wide variety of people running creative companies: 'I'd like to talk to someone who's done it before'. Hearing insights from entrepreneurs who have already navigated the challenges they face can clarify things in a way 20 business consultants would never achieve.

That's really the inspiration for One Thing I Know. We've been lucky enough to meet and work with many intelligent, interesting and inspiring people. We've asked some of them to share their experiences about how they dealt with specific business challenges, the thought processes they went through, how they reached decisions and what actions they took.

Daniel Humphry
Editor

Graduated in '07. Recession in '08. Diminishing freelance rates for years after.

It's a familiar story that many people in their twenties face. Speak to them and you'll soon catch the mood: opportunities are rare and helping hands rarer still. While it would be easy for this 'lost generation' to moan and give up, they've instead done something pretty special.

Small creative businesses are popping up across the country, fronted by recent graduates and freelancers who refuse to sell themselves short. They are producing innovative, trendsetting work and in many areas out-stripping the established agencies who years before had nothing for them.

Inside this book is a mix of young creatives who've made a go of it, and established creatives who wish to share their experience. Hopefully it can be of help.

Dave Sproxton
Executive Chairman
Aardman

These days the word 'innovation' is heard in almost every conversation about business.

It is the buzz word of the day, but for me it should come with a warning note: 'Beware of Innovation for its own sake; can you make your new idea pay its way?' So many pioneers are lost to history simply because they couldn't find a way to make enough money from their idea to make a living. The people we remember, the Edisons and the Marconis of this world, are remembered because they took ideas and made a business out of them. The ideas they used may not have been original but they knew how to raise money, how to market their ideas and how to cut a deal. With the money they made they could re-invest and develop their ideas further. This is the key to successful innovation and entrepreneurship; the ability to develop a business model and sustain income from it.

In an age where more and more people are going to have to create their own job and drive their own income, the skills of entrepreneurship are becoming increasing critical. No longer can it be left to someone else to take care of the business; people are going to have to do it themselves, and in an increasingly complex world. In this context, this book makes a very valuable contribution, being derived from a series of talks and masterclasses delivered by successful entrepreneurs as part of the iNets Innovation Programme. Learning from others and their mistakes is so much better than struggling on your own and making many mistakes along the way. So much of what we know, we have learnt from others, and the skills of entrepreneurship are no different. This book is a valuable tool to help drive success for all budding entrepreneurs.

Contents

Get Up & Go

Strategy

Identity

Getting Noticed

People

Money

Branching Out

Decisions Decisions

Year One : Starting from Scratch

Tim Trusler, Barry Wilkinson & James Lyon
Episode Three

Since founding in 2011, the team at Episode Three have provided exciting marketing and communications films for the likes of Lloyds Banking and Netcomm.

We were probably like a million other creatives across the country. We had all the ideas for starting our own business but were financially comfortable working for someone else. Well, the push we needed came in late 2011 when our employer was forced to call in the liquidators.

The three of us realised that now was finally the time to jump ship and create our own company, and with that Episode Three was born. Like anyone who's lost a full time job, we of course worried about money, but above all it really just felt like the start of a new chapter – a world of new possibilities. We managed to hold onto some of our previous employer's clients and those few jobs gave us an important boost in the first few months. Unfortunately, these clients were having problems of their own, with budgets being dramatically slashed, and so we were pretty much down to a portfolio of zero within a few months; precarious to say the least! That left Episode Three in a tight spot, just two months in but it also taught us to cast your net wide and not rely on a single cash cow - a lesson that is now serving us well.

So, as you might imagine we were far from cash rich in those early days and were the classic tale of starting a company on a credit card. We were actually offered investment from an external party, which was incredibly tempting. However, the sum involved was outweighed by the equity we'd be losing. The words of our business mentor, "giving equity is like pulling teeth," rang in our ears and so we politely declined the cash injection. The decision felt right as angel investors are in it to make money, not friends, and we felt that could be a risk; but right or not the decision didn't exactly help our cashflow situation.

Fortunately, what we did have was a good relationship with the bank and through perseverance we managed to secure a modest small business loan. While it would have been easy to rush out and buy shiny new toys, we were careful not to go over the top with it; keeping the loan to essential business development, and to a size we could pay back even if Episode Three didn't take off.

Our goal then became using that cash to find new clients. We were confident that Episode Three could win them and that all we needed was time to research the market and make contacts. Finding new clients is a long game of course, and so as well as meeting with potential new customers we also continued to spread the word via all our old industry contacts and friends. We found that the best route to any client is peer recommendation and although it has taken time for that initial investment to pay off, we're now winning new customers from marketing efforts started a whole year ago.

—

Like anyone who's lost a full time job we of course worried about money, but above all it really just felt like the start of a new chapter

—

Episode Three has now been in existence for one year and, yes, it has been a rollercoaster. We've won some great clients but also had to hold our nerve when hurdles were looming on the horizon. Ask any start-up in any industry and the story will probably be similar, a first year mixed with fear and massive victories. After learning the risk of cash cows early on our goal now is to keep expanding the client base and win ever more rewarding work. Will that happen? Well, let's just see what the rest of 2013 has to offer...

Ideas are the New Craft

Dave Sproxton
Aardman

Founded by Peter Lord and David Sproxton, Aardman is one company that requires little introduction. Whether in feature film (Pirates!) or commercial advertising (Change4Life) the team has been pioneering West Country creativity over the last five decades.

I'm probably discussing start-ups 30 years too late. Everything was very different when we started, not easier or harder, but different.

While the market was smaller 30 years ago there were also fewer players. Now you have to jostle among a very crowded sector.

From a technique standpoint, it was certainly harder to be a part of the creative industries back then - and not as many people did it. There were only a small handful of companies producing stop frame commercial work; it was a very specialist field. These days, however, technology has allowed such work to become a much more simple process and so competition has boomed.

As such, the skill now is not in the technique of producing a piece of work but in having the idea for it, and that is the difficult part. For example, when the Avid editing suite first came out it cost about £32,000 and that price made digital editing a very specialist activity. In 2013 you can download an Avid app for your iPad and it costs three quid! Ok, it won't have the full facilities, but anybody can create a pretty reasonable video on it. The costs to deliver high quality technical work have absolutely plummeted. You could leave your office right now, walk to Currys and purchase the same cameras that Aardman use for Hollywood-funded films!

Technology has completely levelled the playing field and there's no longer an advantage in (to quote a Marxist line) 'owning the means of production' as the required technology costs next to nothing. Of course, you have to be able to use those tools but it is the compelling, marketable ideas that will stand out.

Nowadays, the creative industry is constantly evolving its production methods to become more efficient, effectively demanding more for less, year-on-year. Every company now needs to give the creatives, who are working on the bleeding edge, the most efficient and effective tools to support their work flow. That is a must because the market is well aware of your competitors, and will be measuring your efficiency against them. That's not just against your peers in the UK either; it could be against a graphic designer in his bedroom in Laos or an agency with 1,500 employees in China. What this means is that the market wants to see more before investing. For creative companies this should raise the question 'How

much work should you be completing up front?' Do we complete a full pilot or just two sheets of paper? And of course, there's no one size fits all answer. What we have learnt at Aardman is to junk weak ideas very quickly. If it's not right then we get out right away and just move on to the next one.

Every creative in every discipline believes they have that one golden idea but, with the proliferation of the sector, in reality there is a good chance that it has already been developed. Just look at zeitgeists in animated film, Antz and Bugs Life, Sharks Life and Finding Nemo. That applies across all the creative industries.

When it comes to technical advances and tools, we find that if somebody has already developed a tool similar to something we were developing, we'll look to partner with them and develop the tool together. That way, instead of building something from the ground up, with high overheads and against an existing competitor, we will have a natural collaborator and a model that is cost effective.

With those partnerships the risk is split and we can be left to concentrate on our area of expertise, safe in the knowledge that the other company is doing what they do best. With new ideas it all comes down to how much money you want to burn and at what stage you wish to bring in

financiers. Start-ups probably have five pounds in their pocket and need to spend every penny on the one idea that might launch them. The key is to gently test the market at each stage so as not to waste all of your money, but you need to understand that you will lose some of it. They say that with advertising half your money is wasted - the trouble is you'll never know which half.

However, with creative work you will know because it'll be sat in a bin underneath your desk! But having said that, out of the ideas that don't work others will fly. You have spin-offs of sorts, and then it's just about knowing how much of your idea to develop before calling in the financiers. Unfortunately that's the $64,000 question to which I have yet to find an answer.

Dividing Your Time Between Creativity and Business

Ross Cleaver
Revolting art and design

Award-winning creative agency Revolting asks its team to look at projects with fresh eyes, and in doing so has produced unique work for the likes of The National Trust and Corfe Castle.

When I was at school I never knew what I wanted to do. I saw Top Gun and I wanted to be a fighter pilot. I saw All Creatures Great and Small and thought I'd be a vet. I've always been able to imagine different scenarios in quite fanatical detail, which I guess was the route to creativity.

I got to sixth form and the teachers said to do what you're good at, so I studied science and art but realised that science was much harder, and slowly dropped everything but art. That led to art college and then university, still with no real job in mind. Then, when my girlfriend at the time was studying graphics, somehow I managed to sit in on her lessons. There was never an end goal in sight, I just kept following all my little interests and before I knew it I was a digital designer.

After a few years in industry the big question became: 'do I work for others, freelance or should I just start my own company?' By then, I felt I'd learnt enough to make it on my own and so I started Revolting. We moved in to my partner's parents' house and just set up in a back room - emailing people and saying we want to work with you. Suddenly, without even realising it I'd become a businessman. The trouble was I was still thinking like a designer.

We thought we could handle both the accounts and the design, and that there'd be no difference between the management and the creative. I was due a rude wake up call! Dividing my time between 'being creative' (actually designing work) and maintaining the accounts and admin of the business became very tricky, very quickly. Every day I handled the pitching, admin and invoicing for each client, but found there was less and less time to carry out the creative. It got ridiculous, to be frank. It peaked when I only had one day a week to create work and was spending the other four talking to printers, sorting accounts, meeting with bank managers etc.

I felt like I wasn't giving the client what they had signed up for. We were selling ourselves as a creative agency and yet the important part of the project, the creativity, was being rushed in at the end of the week. It reached a point when I wouldn't sit down to design until 8pm, and only then because the banks and printers had shut.

Switching between the mind-sets of designing and managing a business, usually back and forth within a day, is not an easy feat. When you're designing, there is often a linear process to creating work. You can concentrate on moving from step to step, but when you're managing a business the work is forever changing. You might start a day with a to-do list, but you'll soon receive a phone call and have to fire-fight that issue. And it's all happening at the same time!

It sounds odd, but one of the ways I handled this was to have two desks. I'd sit at a desk with a computer to handle business issues, and then I would move to one with no computer or phone, take out some pens and just design. That way I didn't have the distractions of urgent emails or nagging phones calls and could focus on trying to be 'creative'.

Even then it is difficult to focus. The emails might not be popping up but the business issues are still in the back of your mind. Eventually, I admitted that you need to separate out each role and have a different individual committed to it, so I bit the bullet and hired somebody to undertake the admin. While this has freed me up to be creative, the reality is that, if you start a business, you'll never just be a 'creative' again. Running the company has become less and less about designing now that I have a team who can realise our creative ideas to a better standard than I ever could. Instead my role is to give creative leadership, to share my ideas and ensure that our work stays in line with the original concept throughout.

The divide between creative and business management is still there, but now I've learnt to step back from aspects of the creative process and to trust my designers. That means I can hand over a creative idea, go take care of some banking issues, and come back to the creative process knowing it is cared for. Getting the balance between being creative and being the businessman is pivotal in running a business like ours and is something that every start-up needs to figure out.

Work vs Life: Taking The Leap

Sally Kenchington
Brightside Films

Brightside Films started in 2010 with the aim of helping creative, talented people win the film or TV commission that they deserve. Since then the team have produced series for the Discovery Channel and Channel 5.

About a year ago I was given a great piece of advice, "do you want to run your company or do you want your company to run you?"

At first, I didn't know what my business mentor meant by this, but after taking a long hard look back over the last two years of running Brightside Films, I had to admit, my company was running me.

Before starting Brightside I spent many years working in television; gainfully employed as part of the production crew. I remember one project I was working on as an assistant producer in which I had a clear sense about how some of the programmes could develop. Perhaps I caught my boss on a bad day, but she made it very clear that I'd crossed a boundary to 'producer level' and would be better off sticking to my role as an 'assistant'. I felt deflated but not defeated because I knew I had it in me to make good programming decisions. Six short weeks later I was offered an amazing commissioner job and bizarrely one of my first assignments was to sign off a project that this woman had produced. I ended up being her boss for a few brief and rather amusing days! It was a valuable lesson and it's led me to follow my gut instinct at every opportunity.

So after this rather interesting twist of fate, I became a full time commissioner for a UK broadcaster in London. The only spanner in the works was that I lived in Bristol. I spent the next year yo-yoing up and down the M4, living in cheap hotels and often working 16 hour days. To say my work-life balance was a tad out of kilter would be an understatement, but I loved my job, my inspiring bosses and the exciting, fast-paced environment – so I wasn't sure what to do!

Then it dawned on me that perhaps I should start working 'with' broadcasters, instead of 'for' them. Sure, being your own boss would come with its own pressures and nerve wracking moments but the idea of setting my own schedule, working on projects that I chose (and with people I respected) was incredibly appealing. I knew this kind of opportunity wouldn't come around again and so it was now or never.

But where to start? I decided to seek as much advice upfront as I could, and was pleasantly surprised that it only cost me about £200 to hire a business professional to set up Brightside Films as a limited company. Within weeks I was registered with Companies House, had said 'hello' to the VAT man and hired a hard working accountant. Money well spent!

Prior to setting up Brightside I'd always assumed I would work well on my own - I liked the feeling of not needing anyone else to get a job done and for a while it worked well. That assumption was challenged when one of my clients broke a contract we had previously agreed. I became unstuck as I didn't have anyone to lean on for advice. I didn't have the cash flow to spend on expensive lawyers nor the inclination to cause a confrontation.

It was a horrible situation to be in, but the silver lining was that it finally forced me to find support, in the shape of a fantastic business mentor. After a few discussions we soon discovered a solution and the dilemma was over. It was a sobering moment and I've made sure to always have proper business support ever since.

Since then I have established a strategy group of around five colleagues who meet every eight weeks. We catch-up, discuss our dilemmas and over two or three hours get the opportunity to help and be helped. It's important to choose trustworthy advisors for this and be confident about where your information is coming from, but it's a good way to remain supported without spending huge amounts of money.

It's exciting times because I feel I'm now firmly in the driving seat of Brightside Films and running my business in the way that's right for me. I'm not growing too quickly or too slowly, I'm working at my own pace and, although it's sometimes stressful, I love it!

Making Fun Pay

Simon Evans
Slingshot

If open city games, in which you're chased through abandoned car parks by rampaging zombies, sound like your cup of tea then take a look at Slingshot - they're the best in this quickly emerging market.

Whether it's the first car or the first time socks were peddled, whenever something new comes along it is initially an uphill battle to show people why they should take a look.

Pervasive street games are a new, tentatively emerging creative form and while people seem to love playing them, shaping the commercial potential has been unexpected and at times tough to realise. Some of the challenges we faced were the sort that any new business faces, but the uniqueness of what we do has presented its own set of difficulties. How do you sell something highly novel? How much can you charge? How do you stage an event in a city with little local knowledge and no local partner?

The advice to be commercially successful may seem like stating the obvious, but it is common in the creative industries to hear people say they want to make something 'good', rather than make money. In the current climate, the opportunities to make something 'good' will be far greater if you can achieve commercial success first, as then you can be your own master. We made many

games before we sold tickets for 2.8 Hours Later and while they were successful in some ways, our company had no momentum and was absolutely reliant on meagre funding opportunities. The cash that 2.8 now generates has enabled us to grow as a business but has also allowed us to create new, innovative work.

Surprisingly, we have found that people in the creative industries are actually quite conservative. In these industries it might be acceptable to create new content within the accepted limits of a recognised art form, but questioning how content is presented and the industry itself is often met with indifference or hostility.

2.8 is basically an awesome game of tag with make-up and this lack of technological wow-factor has meant some dismiss the game as no more than a curiosity. We assemble large numbers of people in cities, sell tickets and give them three hours of entertainment with no local infrastructure, partner or patronage. We roll up in a city, stage the game and leave, like a circus. That we are able to do this is entirely dependent on modern digital communication technologies: web-based ticketing systems, social media and collaborative working. It's a similar story to the virtualisation of the record, print and film industries, where content publishers are no longer dominant. These are very exciting times as nowadays you

can find your own an audience, make stuff for them and they'll pay you directly. You don't need to ask anyone's permission.

Of course we had to start somewhere and engaging friends in our idea, or making new ones around our proposition, meant that we could build a loyal community. All of our first city-wide games were created in an amazing effort by a large number of Bristol's creative community, coming together to do something cool without pay. This delivered a project at a scale we simply couldn't have achieved on our own, but it also did two other important things: the co-creative process ensured the outcome would be popular (if this number of people like the project enough to get involved, others will), and the community itself created a viral awareness through word of mouth.

This inclusive process combines market research, design and marketing into one big creative process. The hybrid of voluntary and paid work lies at the heart of what we do and delivering it is probably where the main value in our business lies. Just as this model has worked for street games, I've no doubt it could also be relevant to other creative businesses as digital communication technologies and social networks could be used to create communities around any project, be it a book, a TV show or film.

Assuming that your business is about exchanging goods for money, marketing is the same as it has always been: getting people to make that exchange with your business. To ensure that people feel invested in our products we undertake a lot of community building work such as inviting the public to meet us in each city and help plan our game. The regular press, radio and direct marketing is still there too.

If, like us, you have a product that is pretty new and unheard of it is vitally important that your messages are coordinated and consistent across all these different communities and channels. It's all well and good having a blockbuster idea but if nobody can understand it then what's the point!

Going Full Service

Gary Seneviratne
Adido

Since humble beginnings as a sole web designer in Bournemouth, Adido has grown into a multi-service agency with major clients including Honda, Camelot, Orange and Easy Jet.

There's a question whether a company should specialise or remain niche. One way to answer is from your customers' basic supply and demand: tell us what you want and we'll do it. However, that's awfully reactive and perhaps the smarter way is remaining free enough to surf changing waves in the market.

But first, let's go back a bit. Adido didn't start life as a full service agency. Initially we focussed on providing design and build for clients as they were our core talents. For the first three years we offered that one service and it allowed Adido to win regular clients, a stable income and enough resources to begin reinvesting. It was a cost effective way of founding our business and so I can understand why start-ups - even large companies - want to be specialised to one single service.

After several years, however, our market demand started leaning towards multi-service. The recession hitting in 2008 really changed both the landscape and our clients' requirements. From a client perspective, managing multiple agencies is a pain and often they don't have the time, patience or budget to shop around five different agencies for five different disciplines. We saw an opportunity to build closer relationships with key clients and grow alongside them by handling whole campaigns with multiple services.

Going full service reduced the recession's impact on our business. Some agencies might have one very strong service but the market moves so quickly nowadays that, in three years, that service may no longer be in such demand. If 90 per cent of your business is dedicated to one service stream and then it dries up, where would that leave you? Probably up the proverbial creek.

So the transition from single to multi-service seemed obvious and it wasn't as tricky as you might think. As any agency will know, it is all about great people, filling the right skills and getting the right personalities in to the team. In short, developing a culture within the business. Our strategy was to reinvest and so when a new project demanded a new skill, and it fitted with our long-term growth strategy, we hired for it.

We were aware that with all these new services there was a risk of our brand image getting diluted. The last thing we wanted was to be known as an agency which does any old thing. Instead, we took a market proposition that focused on asking clients want they want to achieve, and then deciding which combination of services could accomplish their goal. That's very different from trying to wow a client by claiming you specialise in lots of things. Offering a tailored response that focuses on a client's objectives has helped us maintain that market position, and offering multiple services has allowed us to become a key part of our clients' future strategy.

Once all those different service streams were up and running, we began evaluating them in order to identify trends and help shape our business development. We like to pick apart each one of our services to see which have been the most successful, in terms of reception or finance, and then develop it further. As you grow it's worth remembering that markets change. What you serviced 10 years ago, you cannot necessarily service today and you have to shape your agency accordingly.

Consequently, being multi-service means we are well-positioned to handle market shifts. As we are already touching so many different areas of the marketplace we almost get an early warning and can react quickly. We have a vast array of creatives under our roof, each excited and interested by different things, so if a new software or social platform comes along we can let these different people play around and discover its potential. From there we can see how it fits in to our business and why it might benefit clients. Working in multiple spaces means we can stay on the front foot and constantly evaluate a range of platforms.

If we were to go back to single service we would probably lose a large chunk of our clients as even those who previously wanted one service are starting to ask what else we can do for them. It wouldn't make any sense if we now turned around and said nothing. We'd be missing huge opportunities.

Focusing Your Business Models

Tom Quay
Base

Having recently pared down its business models, the all-new Base is now busy creating innovative digital applications for universities and transport groups alike.

Like most founders of a creative company, I don't have a business background.

Base evolved from my freelancing days. It was 18 months before I hired anyone and even then I still had the mind set and makeup of a freelancer. There was no business direction and we simply took on projects when other companies employed us; adding skills and staff along the way. Business and strategy were not words I put together too often.

It was a vague time. We were happy to help any company with any type of project. It was a handy way to make cash early-on, but it meant Base developed three disconnected revenue streams all working in discord. We were building our own products, we were an agency completing very general work-for-hire and we also undertook white labelling, providing technical resources for other creative agencies.

It's fair to say that for those first three years we weren't particularly clear on our direction. To look back at all the competing streams Base had, it's quite impressive to have stayed alive for so long. The strategy was to develop and sell products, but this was dominated by the need to make the money to pay to do that. Soon, we became a little too seduced by work-for-hire to feed our ambition for own-product development. It devolved into one revenue stream propping up another. The result was that we were burning revenue at the same rate we were making it, and that's no way to get anywhere. There was very little cash in the bank to reinvest in the business, which was stifling our growth and slowing product development. We ended up in the frustrating position where our profitable, exciting projects could only move as quickly as the dull, poorly paid ones.

Happily, salvation came in the form of a business mentor. He showed us how to consider our revenue streams as if they were separate business models. Straight away it became clear that Base was stretched too thin and needed to focus. We knew that developing our own products was the one area we all truly enjoyed and while work-for-hire was bringing in a steady income it meant Base had itself become a commoditised resource. With that model, Base would only ever make money working the hours in a day and it didn't add real value to the brand.

It's not as if we enjoyed work-for-hire projects either. We'd fallen so far down in the design process that effectively there was little creative input. At first I felt anxious about moving to one model. I mean who likes cutting away business? But we knew it was happening for the right reasons.

The result is that Base has refined its proposition. It has given us more time to concentrate on the work that, long term, will really matter for us. The excitement about focussed opportunities has also helped us get away from that mind-set of missing opportunities - that seductive, 'oh we could be doing this or that' thinking. Believe it or not, that in itself has a very settling effect within the business.

So there is now a very clear picture of what Base has to look like in order to support our singular business model.

Unfortunately, one tough decision we made was to cut our junior developer at the beginning of this year. It was a hard call as we are a small group, but to reposition we needed the right skills in the business and so it was best for business. Rather than make the team uneasy, as you might expect from a redundancy, it has underlined a determination in all of us to fully realise the company.

I can't recommend enough the process of refining your business models. You need to be honest and see what aspects of your business are not only the most enjoyable, but the most stable, scalable and - most importantly - the ones you are best at. It may seem daunting but really it's as simple as fixing a rate, chasing that work and turning down all the other tempting, but frustrating, projects which shouldn't really be in your business anyway!

The Benefits of Staying Small

Rich Wilson
Mobile Pie

After starting straight out of Bristol University the Mobile Pie team were quick to make their mark with unique, iTunes charting games such as the childhood throwback Top Trumps Collection.

Say what you like, but size matters. Show me a Coca Cola ad campaign under £100m or a Tarantino film under three hours and I'll retract that; but you won't.

The thing is, size isn't the same as quality. There's an unwritten pressure in business that every company must grow. That's what economics dictates and how business management is taught, but of course management practice is devised by accountants, not people motivated by creativity. If you're motivated by quality, what's the right thing to do?

In the games industry, things have changed massively since the introduction of the smartphone. While a console game still needs a warehouse full of talent to produce it, a team of three can develop a mobile game that could rake in millions. This gives a company like Mobile Pie the freedom to ask what size of company do we want to be, especially if we can remain small and still be able to generate a good profit.

More importantly the answer reflects who we want to be and what we want to do. What type of company are we? Staying small allows Mobile Pie to react very quickly to new trends, perhaps quicker than some of the big companies. Large companies with huge work flows are likely to be entrenched in a set way of working but, by their nature, small companies are used to moving from new project to new project, innovating along the way. I'm not saying that big companies can't react quickly to new trends, but suddenly they've got their work flows filled up for the next six months and they simply don't. This is where we little guys can flourish.

Being able to react quickly is a real positive in the mobile games market as it is still young and a bit of a Wild West. You're still never quite sure what will work, and there's

technology to keep up with all the time. At Mobile Pie this means we must to be able to experiment and, unless you have a very forgiving client, that means practising on your own IP. It seems that smaller companies are much more likely to allow a few of their developers an afternoon off to go create a cheeky game, and that means continually experimenting in a very creative way.

However, being smaller we do have to be realistic when we're pitching against larger competition. We can't claim to compete with their staff rosters or budgets. We can't say we have a longer track record or better contact list. What we can do, though, is put forward a pretty risky, leftfield idea to get noticed. Larger companies will tend to propose similar solutions again and again because that's what they understand, and there's a risk of them appearing stale. We try and exploit that by being more nimble and taking the risk of pitching a big, creative idea.

Another clear advantage is the personal touch we can boast. A client will often be dealing with our founders, whose passion for the work should shine through in comparison to yet another account manager. It's simple stuff but if you're a group of five, even a small job is likely to consume most of your time. That is not something a large company can even begin to claim. However, back to the quality issue again, the people commissioning you are often more concerned that you deliver a project on-time rather than you deliver it perfectly. Larger agencies will have dedicated project managers to ensure that happens, so we've had to learn to stress that we have processes in place to match them. Being 'pro-small' doesn't mean you can't grow your profits either.

—

Staying small allows Mobile Pie to react very quickly to new trends, perhaps quicker than some of the big companies

—

In being small, focused and building a great reputation you should be able to grow your business perfectly well from lower overheads and better margins. Digital distribution has really opened up the global marketplace for creative. With very little effort we have learnt to sell our products around the world – avoiding that trap of thinking because you're small you can't compete on a global playing field. In the connected world small can be big business if you're able to find your niche.

HE'S
GOT HIGH
APPLE PIE,
IN THE
SKY
HOPES

How Different is it Running a Larger Agency?

Andrew Henning
Redweb

Redweb is a digital agency that puts a large focus on its people, which is fortunate as in 15 years the company has grown from a single shareholder to a staff roster of nearly 100, with clients such as the RNLI and Sky.

Despite running an agency for 15 years I have yet to reach the stage where any plans from one year to the next are identical. They're rarely even similar! As the agency has grown, my role has had to evolve and it often seems that no one week is the same as the previous. In fact it sometimes feels like I need a new job description every 12 months!

So what is the difference now to when we were 20 staff? Well the first is the sheer quantity of work we undertake. I used to know every job, every customer and status. This is no longer possible and so, in the modern Redweb, reporting is vital, with the process to organise and schedule work (at a profit) increasingly complex. As the business has evolved over the years, we've placed much greater importance on the people who control our day-to-day activity.

As an agency grows, your management tiers must develop too. We have been through a number of changes over the years and have the tremendous advantage of a committed senior level. The grand scheme is that the senior tier is no longer scheduled for client work, allowing them time to plan their departments and manage the needs of their staff.

The larger we have grown, the greater our potential peaks and troughs of profit and loss have become. As the agency has broadened its services, we have seen greater specialism of roles and less opportunity to spread projects across non-specific teams. If all departments are busy then profitability is fantastic but if no one is busy, the salary bill and fixed costs can be daunting.

Despite this, I don't think my stress levels have changed much. When the agency was smaller, issues that arose were generally things that I could solve personally. I was also in a first-hand position to foresee things and prepare the business to react. These days, however, I am normally faced with challenges that have escalated. Here it is important to ensure you have continued confidence in those around you. Jumping to conclusions or acting the hero is not helpful.

To have confidence in your team is vital, once you grow to a certain size. Trusting others, delegating and then realising they can do it better than you, is a rewarding experience. Taking yourself out of every loop is difficult at first, but reducing the number of emails that you're CCed in is a virtue we all should learn.

Finally, does culture need to change as you grow? I'd say that it is impossible for a large agency to have the same culture as a smaller one. But that doesn't mean it has to be worse. In fact, it should be better. The difference with a larger agency is that it needs to be worked at a lot harder to succeed, because with so many people, you can't generate a culture by just going to the pub after work.

—

Jumping to conclusions or acting the hero is not helpful

—

At Redweb we need to work hard to inspire people at the agency both at departmental and discipline levels. We know everyone is busy and we can all suffer from a 'head in the project' mind-set. However, providing opportunities to look beyond the current piece of work gives the agency vitality, independence and a sense to express its own personality.

So would I go back to smaller version of Redweb? No. I personally relish the unknowns that come with continuous growth. Our boundaries are currently only limited by our ability in getting the best people, delivering the best work for the best clients, in the best possible environment.

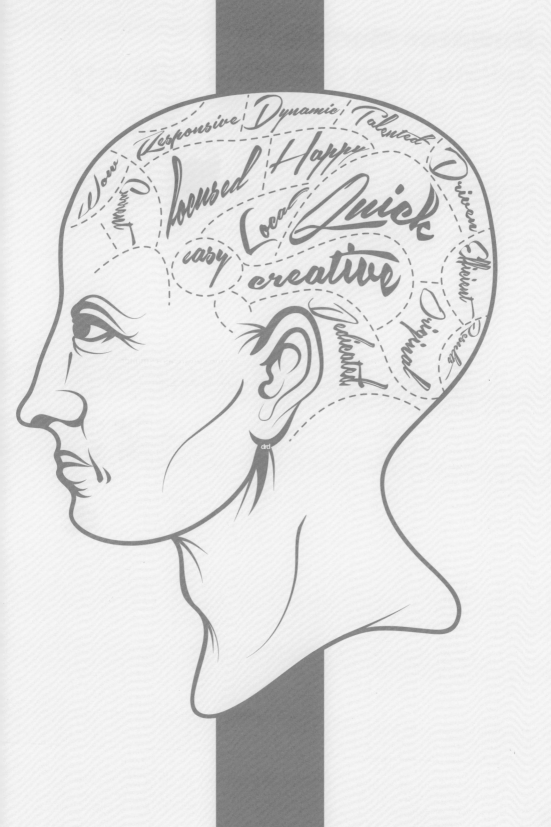

Business Models:
Selling Time vs Selling Products

Ella Romanos
Remode

In the five years since launching, Remode has straddled work-for-hire and IP to launch over 30 games; including the innovative, heart-powered shooter Sky Cycle.

Despite the common perception that there is an infinite number of options when starting a business, there are only really two choices in the creative industries.

The question that any budding entrepreneur needs to ask themselves is: did I want to fulfil client briefs (work for hire) or build my own products (intellectual property)? Essentially, the argument between creating your own intellectual property (IP) and work-for-hire is one of risk versus reward. Work for hire is low risk, but low reward. You know that you will get paid if you deliver on a pre-agreed contract, but your profit margins will always be limited. If you're lucky, then over time you can end up with 20-30 per cent net profit, but it's unusual to get beyond that; and some companies make no profit depending on what their costs are. While a company which only undertakes work-for-hire has no real value outside the business, it can be a robust venture which earns good money for the owners. Still, there is unlikely to be an exit strategy because few people would want to invest in a work-for-hire business.

However, creating your own products is high risk as there's a chance that you'll invest time as well money and the project will fail. Companies who create products are tied to their offering and if that fails, the company fails. That said, if it succeeds the profit you can make is essentially unlimited and not at all proportional to the amount of money put in. Successful IP also gives you great options for exit strategies such as being acquired or merging.

Every company that I've known has made a slightly different decision on which model, or split of models, to follow and there is no right or wrong way. As a business owner you must decide what sort of company you want, what risk you are willing to take and where you want to end up. When we started Remode, we realised that we wanted to build a robust business, but we also wanted to create our own games and build a company that one day might give us a good chance of exit. Essentially, we love making games, but we also love the business and take pride in its growth and want to make profits. Not all creative businesses feel like this. Some prioritise the making of their games over the business, and some are all about the business. We felt we were somewhere in the middle.

On that basis, we decided that the best route was to build a sustainable, profitable business through work-for-hire, and then once we had reached a position where our team was big enough to splinter, we would start creating our own games and taking part in revenue-share partnerships. That way, we would ensure that the business could sustain IP and that the business wouldn't fail if we didn't succeed in making revenue from them. This is probably quite a common model in the creative industry, where some of the more mundane work-for-hire can fuel passionate, expensive IP work. It's not all one way, however, and we have found that, once a company produces a successful piece of IP, client work will come knocking.

—

Essentially, we love making games, but we also love the business and take pride in its growth and want to make profits

—

It took nearly five years to get our studio in a position stable enough to begin creating our own games. After this we had to think carefully about which model, or combination of models would work for us. The most important aspect we had to look at was stakeholder consensus, because changing models later on means fundamentally changing the business and that is not an easy thing to do. If you put off choosing, the likelihood is that your business won't succeed because you won't know what your goals are, and you won't understand what decisions to make or what you need to do to achieve them. You can be cautious but you can't hold off making a firm decision forever.

Getting on with Business

Mark Mason
Mubaloo

Mubaloo has taken the same creative-business approach to apps as founder Mark Mason's previous venture, Mason Zimbler, took to advertising; and in four years has produced work for the likes of The Met Office, BP and William Hill.

People might like to demonise the 'suits' from the 'creatives' but, in reality, business and creativity can co-exist quite nicely if you just get a grip.

There's nothing worse than walking in to a shop and being confronted with a million different types of product. You wonder why the shop exists, what is its purpose? Well, the exact same thing goes for agencies. I see too many small creative agencies trying to be anything and everything to all clients. They do too much: design, apps, brochures, video. It's too broad and it's bad for business because when you become non-specific your marketing spend becomes a drop in the ocean. There's no way you can hit an audience that wide, you'd need a budget the size of a multinational!

Now, marketing yourself might be a dirty concept among creatives but unless you've got clients banging down your door then it's necessary. Marketing has been the lifeblood of my agencies; it's meant that when one of our big clients leave we are in a position to quickly win new business. Any company, creative or not, should have a refined proposition and know how to sell themselves. That's not dirty – that's reality.

When first opening shop, the name of the game is defining your agency. Bizarrely, many creatives fall into the trap of thinking that means producing stand-out project after stand-out project, irrespective of whether they turn a profit. After you've taken the decision to set up a business, you can do that once or twice but afterwards every piece of work should make you money or else you'll end up as busy fools. Otherwise, what are you in business for? Start-ups in the creative world often feel as though every piece of work has to be award-winning. That's wrong, maybe 20 per cent has to be award winning and the rest has to be profitable. Churn it up, get it out the door and make money on it. Those jobs help fund the award winning pieces which, due to the extra time and creative they require, probably won't make much profit themselves.

That's not to say any of my companies have ever set out to create poor work. It's always to a standard, but we only ever really push the boat out when you have a client who has financially afforded you that luxury. You might be a creative but you also have to realise that you're in business to make money. If you make money you can grow and that enables you to go off and be more creative. There are so many two-man bands who don't get that; they never grow and normally shut up shop around year two.

It all really depends on who you fit in to your organisation and what it is you want out of business. For many the ambition isn't to grow but to survive with a lifestyle company - and that's fine. If you want to grow, however, you need to decipher who the profitable clients are; and in my experience they are not always the most creative ones. We keep time sheets for every job we undertake and at the end of the year it becomes crystal clear that 20 per cent of our projects weren't profitable, they were underfunded and expected too much.

One popular argument for undertaking unprofitable work is that it might get you a great brand's badge on your website but, really, how great is a company if they can't even pay full rate? And do you really want to take the risk of bringing on 10 staff for a supposed 'great, creative project' only to have no wages for them come month's end? How much is that badge really worth?

I'm never worried when we turn away business over price issues because we price our margins accordingly. If we then lose work because somebody has undercut us, then I'm confident that they're not going to make money. If that's how they do business then they won't grow and thus are not a competitor to me. They can do what they like.

CREATIVE THINKING
IN BUSINESS

THE BIG BOOK OF TAX

HOW TO BE A GRAPHIC DESIGNER

PANTONE
172C

Can a Successful Business Create Fun Stuff?

Ben Templeton
Thought Den

Thanks to their focus on fun and creativity, Thought Den has produced everything from web games to magic eight balls for major arts institutions including The Science Museum and Tate.

I'm sure many people have grand claims about why they started a business.

Creative vision, a million in the bank, world peace and all that. My reason was that I had fun working with a friend and, really, what better reason could you ask for?

Focussing on fun has meant that while Thought Den has remained a relatively small agency, we have also gained a reputation for producing creative work. Somehow fun and creativity became our business strategy, not that we'd call it that, and this is how we produce work we're proud of.

Of course, setting out to remain creative is all well and good but you need clients who also appreciate that sort of thing. In the early days we were taking what scraps were offered to us and trying to have fun with them. Gradually, as our skills improved, we became more discerning. We were working with Jack Daniel's and Southern Comfort early on and that's quite different from the arts and culture work that we're doing now. While Jack Daniel's is a great client, there's a different feeling to the job; a shorter life span, less love in the project. The arts and culture sector appealed because the content we'd be working on – art, science, history – is really rich and quite meaningful to people.

What has been fundamental in winning these clients is our enthusiastic approach. We're not hard business people and so we don't act like that. The Tate hired us because they liked our attitude. Maybe if we were selling photocopiers we couldn't be as laid back in how we talk to customers, but the way we present ourselves fits with our work and the industry we're in.

Part of keeping Thought Den personable and fun has meant giving each other flexibility; understanding that if it ever becomes too difficult, or if the work is no longer enjoyable, then we'll simply stop. It's almost like we've got nothing to lose. We've adopted the understanding that life comes first.

While for others that might sound a ridiculous business philosophy, I have faith that if Thought Den did close, all of us here are talented enough to go on to better things. Without getting too philosophical, we've had so much fun getting to this point and learnt so much, we can't lose. I wouldn't mind a bit more money in my pocket to show for it but we're working for some incredible brands, so it feels like every week we're winning in other ways.

Once you realise closing the business isn't the end of the world it liberates you as a company. You no longer take on the awful projects just to stay alive and instead can take risks, you dare to create something different. It is only when you're free to make those leaps that something impressive can be created, not when you're churning out websites ten-a-penny.

When we started out, we didn't say 'right we want a £4 million company, 20 employees and an office in a skyscraper - we just said we want to make cool work. What we wanted to achieve was flexible enough that we feel like we're winning with every step forward, though sometimes the creative and business aspects of Thought Den are almost in opposition with one another - and that has been an on-going issue.

In the early days we weren't fussed about growth but on reflection it's now clear that our desire to 'be creative' often means we're over-delivering. While that's a good way to create an impressive portfolio, it's no way to build toward the future. We're in a position now where we're working with great brands on fairly big budget projects, and if someone was to invest 50-100 grand we could take it to the next level very quickly. We'd probably all start earning some proper money too.

However, the question is, 'how big do we want to be?' In truth, I'm largely satisfied with things as they are. We set up Thought Den both aged 22, just out of university, and now we're employing people – that feels ridiculous. So long as we continue producing work to be proud of, stay creative, and grow a little, I think that should be enough.

Defining a Brand with Integrity

Ben Steers
Fiasco Design

Founded in 2010, Fiasco Design have gone from strength to strength over the past three years. Working with clients such as Channel 4, Aardman, BBC and The Watershed, they were also involved in Nightmare High - the BAFTA award-winning online game from Somethin Else Media.

Who am I? It's one of the easiest questions to ask but one of the most challenging to answer. Even if you can't quite nail it in life, knowing who your business is and keeping its identity consistent is vital.

Like it or not, in 2012 brand defines us and it's essential to establish a strong image if you want to achieve any sort of market position. Three years ago Fiasco approached its brand identity with reluctance and a lack of confidence. We didn't set down any guidelines for our brand approach, such as use of font type or logo, and as a result there was a severe lack of consistency across the branded work we were putting into the digital realm. It looked messy, and I realised that everything you do, inside and outside of work, is a reflection of the business. So I began to look more closely at how to make it work.

We found that you needed four key ingredients: coherence, consistency, legibility and mystery. We were falling down in the first three of these, with the only mystery being that we weren't entirely sure ourselves what we were offering! It's so important to look at what your offering is and the market around you, then set down a clear direction or set of objectives moving forward. These considerations will always start with the same sort of questions. Who are we? What are we going to offer? What are our strengths? The answers to these questions helped inform us about the kind of brand we wanted to create, the kind of identity that we wanted to release into the world. It showed us the type of business we wanted to be.

However, this is all pie in the sky unless you work with clients who match your style. When I left university, I was told that the best path of action would be too take on any work I could find, initially just to build up my experience and portfolio; even if that meant working for free. I don't want to discourage this entirely, but I do think that you have to set yourself a standard.

Sometimes we'll work with clients who, while they can't match our full rates, we admire and want them on our portfolio. Sometimes they can make up for costs with the added exposure or services trade they can offer. Just last year we worked on a new website for Alfresco Disco knowing full well that the budget wasn't going to stretch,

ut we took it on anyway because we like what Alfresco do, like their brand and the events they put on. We felt hat the reduction in cost would be justified by having a brand like theirs on our books.

—

However, this is all pie in the sky unless you work with clients who match your style

—

The key point is about integrity and to value your own work. Design has become an undervalued part of what businesses do these days. Adverts for 99p logos and websites for £200 have meant that everyone thinks they can get design work for peanuts but as everyone knows 'pay peanuts, get monkeys'. It is very easy to get frustrated with this, especially in the early days, but while you shouldn't rule anything out, you also shouldn't take any job at any cost just because your bank balance is low. Integrity is such an important aspect of business.

If you want to build a successful brand it's going to take time and people have to believe in what you're doing before they place trust in your business. That is a lot easier when you have a portfolio of creatively interesting, authentic work. When you're trying to make this a reality, mistakes are inevitable but that is just part of the learning process and you can't be afraid to try new things.

Unfortunately, we live in a culture where mistakes are seen as an indication of failure and discouraged from school and beyond. But without making those mistakes, how do you ever learn? We decided that if we stayed completely within our comfort zone we'd put out mediocre, forgettable work. Our ethos has been: step outside your comfort zone, be bold, be daring. Be offensive if you have to be! We'll learn more about ourselves that way than always taking the safe option.

Shedding Your Artistic Pretentions

Louis Jones and Dylan Shipley
Sun & Moon Studios

After shunning the tropes of an artist in favour of agency life, the Sun & Moon founders have gone on to create bespoke animation, design and interactive content for the likes of the BBC and E3.

How important is artistry?

Being 'creative' is a big reason for people to join this sector, but for a business it's not always practical. Take the animation industry, for instance. There are essentially two paths you can take when starting out as an animator. One is to be a filmmaker, to create subjective art and show it around the film festival circuit. The other is to build up the skills required to become a crafts person, and to ply those skills in the creative industries.

We have pretty much always seen ourselves, at least professionally, as craftsmen. That means our business and creative have to go hand-in-hand and means we can't see ourselves as purely 'artists'. Sure, we love what we do and want to create something of quality, but we're also aware that we are providing a service to fulfil a brief.

To start on that path as an industry craftsman we had to learn the tools of the trade, and in animation that meant Flash and vector-based artwork. Now that might seem like an obvious thing to anyone in the sector, but 90 per cent of our paying animation work requires those systems and yet only 10 per cent of people coming in to the industry seem to know them. Perhaps there's been too much of a focus on the artistic side of making animation as opposed to the craft side of knowing your trade.

In the early days of Sun & Moon we probably acted too much like artists. We were certainly a lot closer to the work we created and invested a lot of ourselves into each project, perhaps too much. We find that creativity is often too precious and taken too seriously. You hear people talking about 'this is my work, this is my style', but we've learnt over time that it is more important to take your ego out of a project. Back then, we fought clients who wanted something from a project which wasn't to our creative tastes, and at times it caused friction because we had too rigid an idea of how a project should be.

This might be a shock, but as business owners it's pretty important to have work coming through the door. Well, for that to happen we need to be pretty open about the projects we consider and to make sure we deliver what they want. It's a tough battle because while you always like a bit of repeat business, you also need to keep your name clean and produce work with creative merit.

In a perfect world studios would shape each and every project in their own vision. However, we've learnt that when a client's mind is made up it's often better to deliver a project as they would like it. That doesn't mean our studio ever compromises on quality – when clients give poor ideas we often suggest a better one, explain it and demonstrate why we prefer it - but ultimately we also remember who is paying who. Whether we like it or not, this is a commercial business and clients are paying for our services. While they might not always be right – they will always have the last word.

This was all part of how we learnt to drop any artistic pretentions. It's a good thing too, because those pretentions can cause you to take your work too seriously and produce projects which are too heavily ego-driven. That type of work won't be right for the client and in this small, word-of-mouth industry; people will soon find out if you've been precious, demanding or inflexible. Word travels quickly and for us a large part of being successful in the creative business has just been being nice.

These days we definitely lean more towards creative business people than artists. We check that a job has either something financially or creatively enticing, ideally both, and then try to balance our creative desires with a client's expectations. That's much harder in the creative industries than in others where owners generally think: 'this pays well so we'll do it, this doesn't so we won't.' There are other factors, for instance a project may pay poorly but bolster your portfolio and help land future work. Really, that just means we now look to hear out all potential projects and not knee-jerk against them as who knows what they could develop into. And above all, we never, ever, let any artistic pretentions lead our business.

Focusing Your Business Proposition

Duncan Cook
3 Sided Cube

While there are many noble goals in the creative industries, 3 Sided Cube's chart-topping Red Cross app has saved countless lives during US natural disasters and took them to the White House in 2012. Top that!

There's a fine line dividing what an agency can do and what it should do.

Let's face it, most agencies could do pretty much anything as once you've grasped the basic concepts of design, interactivity and storytelling, it's not hard to apply them across all sorts of formats. Nowadays the question isn't what can you do, but what should you do?

If your agency isn't focussing on what it offers, you can fast become a classic Jack of all trades. Of course, that's what a lot of businesses want to be, but look at it from your clients point of view. If you're a small company, will they truly believe you can provide all of the design, print, advertising, web, SEO, TV and so on. It's just not viable. For one you won't have the skill set and secondly if you're a small company you won't have the sheer volume of personnel – you'll need to outsource.

If you claim to be doing everything while actually outsourcing, then you'll be competing against the real big players who are slick and full of knowledgeable people. You won't be able to beat these companies on the services you can provide, so then all you can compete with them on is price. If that's all you've got as your USP, then you're going nowhere fast. It's just not sustainable.

Too many companies start out shouting 'we can do the same and we can do it cheaper' but in the creative industries that is a terrible model. Price gives you clients who want everything for nothing. It doesn't give you profitability and it doesn't give you growth.

By focussing on a single or very closed group of disciplines you are able to bang that one drum and focus all of your energy on ensuring that people hear the right message. Soon people will begin to associate you with that discipline and when that happens, when you're already in the back of people's minds as a 'specialist' in one field, you're already on potential clients horizons. If I was looking for someone to help with SEO on a project, I instantly think of two or three companies who do nothing but SEO. They're the people I would contact. Simply put bang too many drums and your message will get lost in the noise.

Companies need to know what they are good at and find how they can use that talent to differentiate themselves from the competition It might be that you are far more creative than anyone else or that you are very technical. I would say use that; lean on it and go after the appropriate projects. If you establish yourself as known, say, for being very technical, then it will be easy for a more creative-led agency to see the benefit in working with you.

Focusing your discipline goes hand in hand with focusing on how you market yourselves. Small companies don't have huge marketing budgets and it is so much easier to promote yourself when you've only one identity to push By dividing your efforts and your resources between too many specialities you might soon find that your marketing becomes a drop in the ocean. In my experience it is best to focus all that energy, time and money on shouting about one thing.

If you're starting out, you may not yet know which sector or discipline you would like to specialise in. That's fine, carry out a few projects, see which ones best fit your company, which ones you are good at and let it come organically. But when you do find that speciality, you should really jump right on it.

Though 3 Sided Cube started out offering a few different disciplines, it became a no-brainer to pursue just the one. We saw that the app market was growing, had lots of opportunities and so we went after it. Yes, we lost work; we could have taken on lots of work handling web applications as well as mobile, but in the long term it has strengthened our brand within a niche market. In turn this has allowed us to take on large clients like Boots, who would have laughed a small agency like us out the door had we claimed ourselves able to create their site, their mobile, and their advertising. Ultimately, focusing on a single discipline has made our name, won us clients and allowed us to grow.

This book belongs to

& I am
/ we are really
really good at

Developing Products to Build Brand Image

Jim Douglas
Future

Founded in 1985
with just one
magazine, Future
now bestrides
global specialist
publishing with over
200 titles across
the UK, US and
Australia.

Whatever you make, your first product will inevitably influence how others perceive you.

It will help shape your brand. This shouldn't be limiting as you would hope that your first product would embody many of the values or skills that you want associated with your company. Also, that first product can also act as a springboard behind the development of future products.

For example, our very first Future product many years ago was a computer magazine with a cover-mounted cassette tape for Amstrad computers. The fact that it was about Amstrad computers was largely irrelevant from a company brand point of view. What really mattered was the fact it was a specialist magazine with an innovative approach to adding value for its readers - in that case, the tape. That approach helped shape our approach to what came next, and many years on it's been reflected across the majority of Future's products and still helps solidify our brand image.

From the beginning, you need to be thinking about how each product may affect the perception of your brand. You should hope that everything you do contributes somehow to the overall image. For instance, it's important for Future to be seen as a digitally progressive media business with international reach, so if we were going to launch a product that had no digital component and no international potential, would that make sense? Interesting opportunities come up all the time – the discipline is only going forward with those which also contribute to your wider strategy.

Being able to transfer Future's approach across many different sectors has been key for the company. Deciding which markets to engage with, and determining what opportunities are available within them, is a vital step. The way that we have been able to expand is by applying our skills to adjacent sectors. For example, there is obviously a strong affinity between home computer owners (where we started), gamers (where we went next), science fiction and in turn a wider interest in film. So, over the years, we made it our strategy to gain a strong position in one of these sectors and then successively launch in corresponding areas. Similarly, we've a strong and loyal position within the cycling community and that has enabled us to move into the triathlon market. Adjacent diversification has allowed Future to utilise its existing expertise when moving in to new markets and afford itself the greatest chance of success.

The majority of our products help people get more from their hobby or passtime. If someone is interested in cycling then they'll likely be looking for advice on what gear to buy and that means there is an opportunity for our magazine. In general a good approach is to try and identify a problem you can solve for either a consumer or a customer – so in that example; too may products to chose from; and consumers needing trusted advice from credible experts. If you can't identify the problem which either your product or company solves then why should someone need you?

Of course, a major factor of this has been identifying and then gaining the acceptance of new audiences, and it's important to get a handle on your market to judge likely demand. Future spends a lot of time researching potential audiences, which products work for them and how consumer media plays a role in their lives. We create user profiles and user stories to ensure our websites, magazines and events will feel worthwhile and that way we can be confident of success.

These days our portfolio is quite broad, it can be a challenge to work out if some products are 'on brand' – we cater to some very distinct audiences (from video games fans to avid knitters), but the 'way' we cater for them, by trying to create innovative and engaging products with lots of benefits that help them get more from their area of passion – there is more consistency there than you might first think. So considering how the specific product you are working on aligns with your wider approach and reflects your desired brand perception in the eyes of clients, customers and contacts is extremely important.

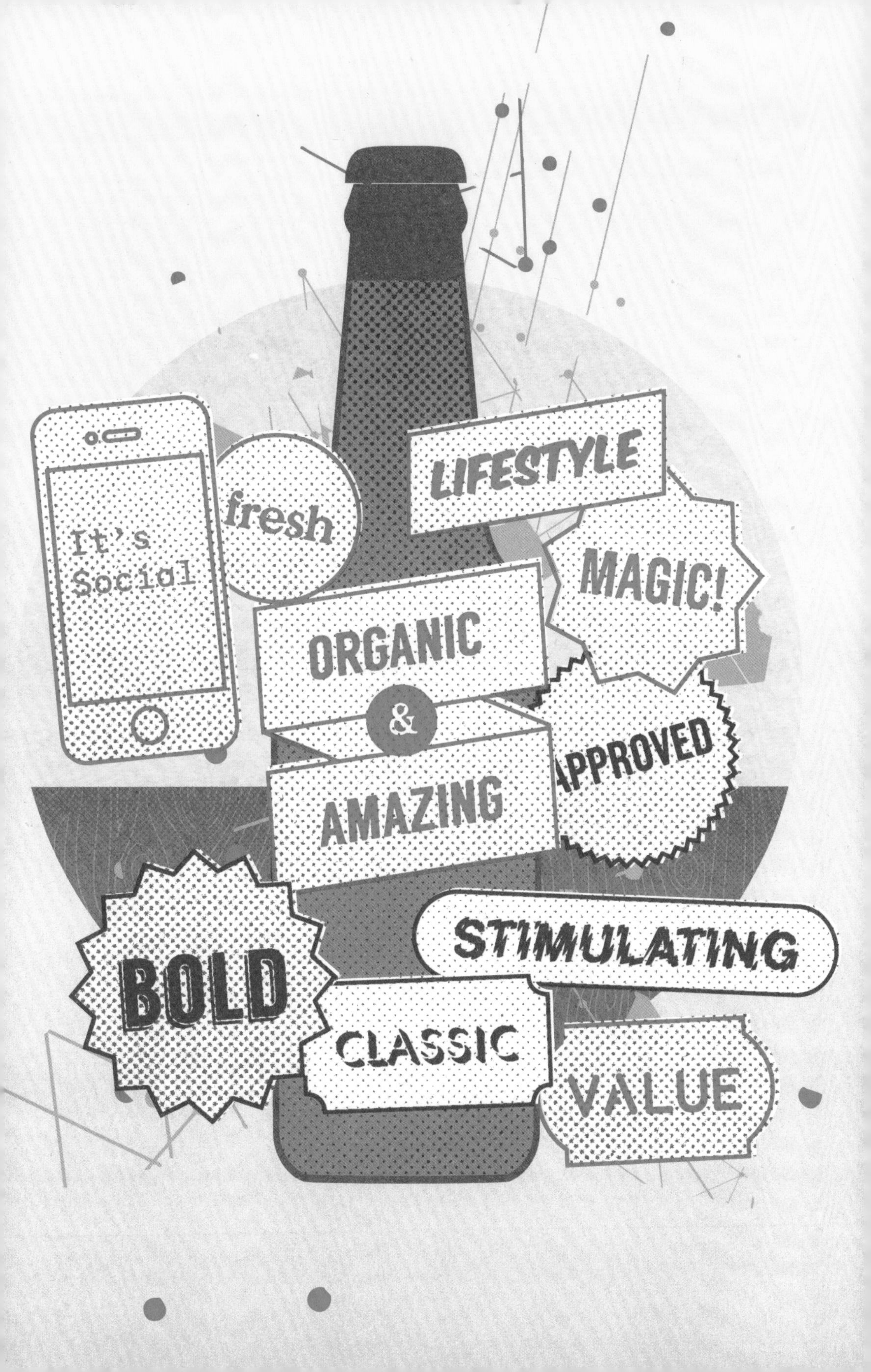

It's Social
fresh
LIFESTYLE
MAGIC!
ORGANIC
&
AMAZING
APPROVED
BOLD
STIMULATING
CLASSIC
VALUE

What's Your Company Culture?

Caroline Hagen
Reach

Brand agency Reach has drawn on its director's diverse backgrounds to develop closer ways of working with – and not just for – their clients; who include New Covent Garden Soups and Air Wick.

'Company culture' sounds like one of those overblown media buzz phrases.

The thing is, nearly every company has one whether they're aware of it or not. As someone who works with brands, I was very conscious that having a set of values, the right atmosphere and a working practice which defined who we were, could make a big difference to Reach when we started. What I was less certain about was how to make that happen.

Initially, I wasn't sure what sort of culture our company should develop and wondered if our values should be set in concrete from day one or allowed to manifest over time. I discovered that it's very hard to impose a culture on a company. It has to radiate from the people working inside it and the best place to start is from the principles of the founders.

I began by asking why we needed to impose a cultural identify. Firstly, I wanted the staff to know what we stood for and what we wanted to achieve. However, having a tangible culture in place seemed even more vital from a client perspective. Without it, how could our company differentiate itself from any other agency? Instead of just relying on our portfolio, having a recognisable company culture gave potential clients a greater sense of who they would be working with. My partner came from a creative design background and I from an account management one. Our separate backgrounds gave Reach a natural democracy between creative and business, and so part of our culture became placing equal importance on both.

While it is easy to talk about the concepts of our company culture, unless it was tangible, the chances were that our employees would never be able to adopt it. We found that the company needed both over-arching values and the nitty-gritty rules of how they should be applied in daily working life. That means actually documenting the company's values and working practices, then making sure they were read and understood. By doing this we avoided so much of the day-to-day micro-management. Employees simply knew what we stood for and how they should go about business.

It was only once our culture could be applied in everyday business that it really started to add value. For instance, one of our core cultures was' collaboration' and we interpreted that on a daily level as not being arrogant to clients and accepting that they have a wealth of knowledge to offer. Today it means we sit down with clients at every stage to discuss ideas - hence our values have determined our procedures.

There's a danger, of course, that having values can restrict progress, so a company culture should be given room to evolve and shift with time. Our first core values – collaboration, democracy, clear wording – were quite nice and quite soft, we were known as a 'nice' agency to work with. After a time, however, we wanted to become more strategic and adopt more challenging behaviour with clients. We wanted to question their motives to develop better briefs, but I didn't think we could do that with our existing values. In fact some staff left because they'd originally joined a softer, nicer culture but we wanted to become harder – and that wasn't for them. During that period our culture required careful handling, but because of that our new philosophy is engrained in the business and we have been able to change and work in a new way. By being clear with our values, staff knew where they stood, which cut down a lot of uncertainty, and moaning.

A properly implemented company culture should help companies develop a well-defined market position. Our values have built the idea of 'co-creation' between us, client and customer – and in effect given Reach its USP. Having that clearly-defined culture has made recruitment and training much easier, it has given us a recognised position within our industry and allowed us to change the whole nature of our business while remaining one and the same. In short, it has opened up new markets and allowed us to keep pace with our competitors. Overall, introducing values has been very beneficial for us – it's certainly not just media hype; but you do need to be aware of what culture you are instilling. The impact can be far reaching.

I'M A

MASSIVE FAN *of*

COLLABORATION

BUT IT ISN'T EASY!

IT TAKES COURAGE TO *share ideas*

AND TO GIVE UP A BIT OF
CREATIVE CONTROL.
BUT WHEN YOU CHOOSE · THE · RIGHT COLLABORATOR

THE RESULTS ☑

TOTALLY JUSTIFY THE RISKS.

SPENCER BUCK | HEAD OF PICTURES
+44 [0]117 973 5151

Nice OF *Spence* TO ASK ME TO HELP HIM WITH THIS *Collaboration* PIECE INSTEAD OF DOING IT HIMSELF

MADE IN BRISTOL ▲ HB

But I GUESS THAT'S THE POINT? REALLY, ISN'T IT

Two HEADS ★ARE★ BETTER THAN *One.*

LINDSAY CAMP | HEAD OF WORDS
+44 [0]786 757 0748

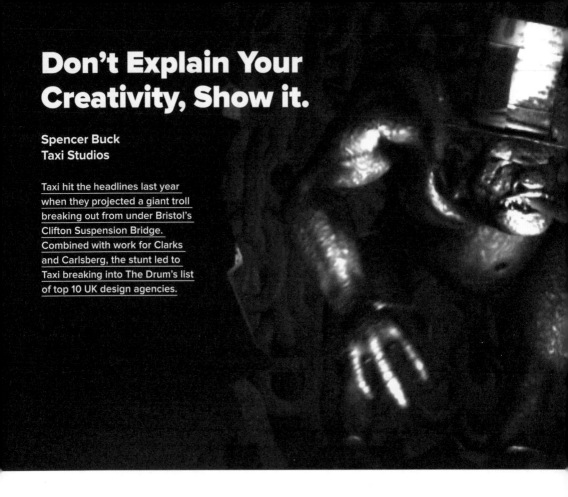

Don't Explain Your Creativity, Show it.

Spencer Buck
Taxi Studios

Taxi hit the headlines last year
when they projected a giant troll
breaking out from under Bristol's
Clifton Suspension Bridge.
Combined with work for Clarks
and Carlsberg, the stunt led to
Taxi breaking into The Drum's list
of top 10 UK design agencies.

Considering how creative we're all supposed to be, it amazes me how uncreative some creatives are when it comes to promoting themselves, or their business.

Every 'considered' marketing communication is vying
for the same attention as everyone else's. It's a simple
principle – if you don't achieve cut through then you're
screwed. Whether promoting your creative business or
answering a client brief, our job is to cut through the
banality, noise and clutter in a way that is interesting
and memorable.

We recently re-branded Taxi's identity to better reflect
our positioning (Fearless Creativity) and, to mark the
occasion, we wanted to create something thrilling.
We didn't think placing an advert in Creative Review
or sending out direct mail was fearless or creative; we
needed an idea that was itself fearless. It was exciting; it
took us back to the early days when Taxi was a fledgling
businesses striving to make a name for itself, much like

start-ups do. Back then the temptation was to make a
big splash in design magazines with expensive 'vanity'
ads but, frankly, that was the wrong approach. Creative
businesses should be pushing boundaries, showing how
different they are; not just claiming it.

I realised that we'd have to do something pretty epic but
on a modest budget; but what? As a proudly Bristol-based
company we've obviously been inspired by Banksy. His work
and balls are profound. Every day we see the Suspension
Bridge from work and I knew something special could
be done there. I was on holiday shortly after seeing the
Jubilee celebration projections on Buckingham Palace and
these thoughts started merging in the back of my mind,
I realised we could use the bridge for some sort of stunt
using these video projection techniques.

It had to be a one-off, guerrilla-style thing and the costs
had to be kept down. That meant developing an idea
others would love and hopefully buy in to. Fortunately,
Play Nicely loved the idea and came on board as digital
partners but we still needed to find video projection
specialists. I trawled the net and struck up a conversation
with a bunch in Essex called CMT. We were a bit cheeky
and opened the conversation with something like: "We'd
love to work with you but your branding and website is

crap." They liked the cut of our jib and so, in exchange for their services, we're redesigning their brand and website. The Troll Bridge could have cost us over twenty grand all in all, but we managed to create this huge viral stunt on a budget that anyone could afford. Even a start-up.

Of course it wasn't without its risks. We didn't have permission for a start. While I was prepared to be arrested for it to succeed, I wasn't prepared to cause any injuries and so we took safety precautions. With these types of stunts you have to ask yourself what level of risk you are prepared to face? I'd quite like to project King Kong on the Empire State Building, but the coppers over there have guns, and litigation is rife, you can get sued for the silliest of things. I'm not in a mad rush to experience their judicial system anytime soon!

Thankfully it all paid off. I didn't get nicked and we achieved major cut through – much more than any advert could ever deliver. By the next morning we'd had over 0,000 views on YouTube, blog pieces from top trade media and emails flooding in. Our aim was to get it on the 0 o'clock news, and by the Friday night there it was on TV. The cherry on top is that Troll Bridge is up for some awards too.

Putting this stunt together was a great reminder to not set a limit on your thinking. A great idea doesn't always need lots of money thrown at it. Work out what you need to make it work and then just get on with it. True creativity doesn't just reside in getting the idea. In fact, that's the easiest bit. It's also about the blood, sweat and tears of bringing it to life and executing it bloody well.

We're in the business of communication. We're in the business of selling stuff to people, extolling the virtues of the client's product or service (or both) to a consumer. If a creative agency can't sell itself well, then what's the chance of them being able to sell anything else?

No matter how many times you blather on about how creative you are or your agency is, whether that's in a line on your website or in an advert – not everybody's going to hear you, see you, or give a shit. I think the point is this: if you believe you are good enough, find inspirational ways to SHOW people, then they'll be more likely to stand up and take notice.

Putting Yourself Out There

James Carroll
Evil Twin

After catching the eye of CBBC and making clients of Adam and Joe with their leftfield animations, Evil Twin have recently turned their vision to the mobile apps market.

At no point while studying to animate gun-headed characters did I think I'd end up spending half my day hustling business development and marketing people.

I don't know about you, but that's not what my animation background trained me for, and I've had to learn on the job.

There's a moment once you get everything set up, you look around the studio and think: right I'm ready for business. Then it slowly dawns on you that nobody's going to come knocking on your door – you're going to have to win business. To begin with I hated ringing people, I had to psych myself up for sales calls. It took ages, but I guess I got used to it. You've just got to bite the bullet, do it or don't.

The most important first step was to get the right people to have a look at our work. This might sound obvious, but there are thousands of creative people wanting to do what we do, and some of them even have the talent for it, so it's the people who make every effort to be seen that will get a break.

We knew that we had to show people what we could do. We looked through every directory and phoned every studio to see if they'd look at our work. We put ourselves out there each and every day and hustled every lead we could find. The rule we followed, and which I think probably applies to any industry, is that it is much easier to grab someone's attention by placing a physical object in their hands. A lot of people send emails with a link to their YouTube show reel. Getting the right person's name and email address is a great start, but emails can so easily be overlooked.

The other rule we followed is that we wanted to reflect 'us' – I don't think we used the word – but we wanted to push a brand and distance ourselves from the hundreds of other show reels that every studio receives. We asked ourselves what is it we really like doing, and what is it these studios really do. The answer to both was telling stories and so it seemed obvious that our show reel should be an animated short story, meaning we'd have a product with some actual legs to it, something that could hold their interest.

This instantly helped us stand out. So many animation companies send show reels which are just abstract snippets of characters or scenery. Again, that's all well and fine but if you're sending it to a company which tells stories for a living it's probably not going to rock their world.

Getting the right response was all about knowing our market and creating something for it. I mean, you've got to question people who send abstract snippets of animation to Aardman. Have they ever seen an Aardman animation? They're certainly not abstract. The point is that our first foray in to the industry came because we created something a bit different, hustled it around mercilessly and fortunately got it front of some very nice people.

As we became that bit more established, 'putting ourselves out there' increasingly meant less time sending products to potential clients and instead attending networking events. What we soon found is that there's an art form to those gigs all unto themselves.

Initially it seemed smart to attend networking events full of like-minded people - animators, illustrators and designers. However, it soon became apparent that the one person who'd actually get any attention was the lawyer in the room. All the animators would just look at each other and say: 'I don't really need anything from you to be honest'. The trick is going to networking events where your skill can fill a gap in the market. There are lots of events that go on for every profession and you should only be visiting the ones where either you can stand out or fill that gap.

What astounded me the most, whether at networking events or when phoning around the houses, is that people liked a chat. When you're starting out it's hard to imagine people will actually hear you out but we discovered that if you just get them outside of that pressurised, business environment then people love a natter. In fact, so many of our business deals have been done down the pub that it's unreal!

Putting yourself out there really comes down to meeting like-minded people that could use your skills and then demonstrating to them why they should go with you. The most important thing we learnt was to take our time and treat that stage of our business with as much care as you would a piece of client work. It can be the difference between making it or not.

YOU SHOULD

ALWAYS

TAILOR

YOUR STORY
FOR YOUR
AUDIENCE

The Pitfalls of Networking

Arabella Lewis-Smith
Salad

While other agencies dub themselves trendy creatives, the Salad team are open about their 'geeky nerdism' and for their honesty have won clients including Salomon and Tigre D'or.

Just over a decade ago I had a degree in fashion and textiles, no agency experience, no clients and absolutely zero business training.

I was basically the person that Dragons Den would have shouted out the room with some combination of the words 'joke', 'delusional' and 'nice girl but...'

Still, start a business I did. My partner and I pooled some money into a bank account, rented a tiny office, designed an identity, cobbled together a brochure and then called everyone we knew. Amazingly, some of those people actually gave us work and our little agency was born.

Soon after this we hired our first designer and while those wonderful friends gave us a little bit more work it wasn't enough to sustain three people, in fact it wasn't enough to support one. In our first year as agency owners we earned virtually nothing, about £5,000 on my part. We needed to generate new business and so we needed to sell. Cripes, I had no experience in selling and after the mates route had no idea where to start.

Our friends advised local networking events but I had never heard of them. Apparently, they were gatherings of business people talking business. The thought of going into a room full of strangers and talking about myself scared the living daylight out of me, but there was no choice; we needed new clients and so I had to give it a go.

I imagined myself breezing in, heads turning with a 'who is this interesting looking person' expression on people's faces. I thought I'd give a short introduction, answer a few questions and, hey presto, I'd have these business people practically begging for my business card. As you might imagine this wasn't the case. In fact, it turned out to be a horrible, toe-curling experience.

What I actually found was a room full of stereotypically suited men. They all looked the same and they all seemed to know each other: photocopier salesmen, accountants and a whole array of (what seemed to me at the time) old, grey, boring, overweight men whom I had nothing in common with. Naturally, I left empty handed and without any of my ridiculous hopes being realised. While perhaps my memories are worse than the event actually was, it shocked me into the realisation that my networking efforts needed a rethink.

My problem is that I had always been shy when it came to discussing myself, and as our company felt like an extension of me, it was something I needed to overcome. Once I realised that it was only my own insecurities that were holding me back, that the people I met generally wanted to hear my story, things got easier. Someone once asked me 'why do you hide your light under a bushel?', which is a really old fashioned term, but for whatever reason it stuck and I realised that no one benefited from shyness disguised as modesty.

—

The thought of going into a room full of strangers and talking about myself scared the living daylight out of me, but there was no choice; we needed new clients and so I had to give it a go

—

One of the most important things I discovered was that my challenge wasn't networking itself but with finding the right people. The fundamental change to my approach was to stop thinking 'what's in it for me?' and instead ask 'what can I do for others?'. This isn't limited to formal networking events, indeed life itself is a networking event, and offering help with no obvious gains for yourself will ultimately come back and reward you. Maybe not from the sources you would imagine, but in my experiences you get back what you put in to a community.

People now tell me I'm a great networker. I'm still no fan of 'business networking' events and tend to find them a tad stuffy, but they have their place and as such have to be included in the mix of business development activities. Still, don't expect to arrive and create a stir; networking requires investment and patience before you build rapports. Now I'm in a position where I've stopped thinking of networking as something confined to your working life and learnt to be open discussing what I do wherever I am. I'm in it for the long game, and happy to have finally figured out how to make networking work for me.

Getting Your Social in Line

Niko Lemanis
Fuel Communications

Fuel's marketing know-how helps other businesses promote themselves effectively. Over the last few years they have worked with clients as diverse as Plymouth Argyle FC and Tamar Science Park.

How weird is it to think that in 2001 direct email was only just becoming recognised as an effective marketing tool?

12 years later it's out of date. What's replaced it is the phenomena called - well if you're over 25 - social media, but if you're under 25, there's no name, really, it's just everyday life.

Despite the domination of the medium – there's still a lot of uncertainty about it and lots of people use it really badly. Ten years ago businesses didn't send out 500,000 direct mail shots explaining what their CEO had for breakfast, so why do they suddenly think that's an interesting topic of conversation for their corporate Twitter account? Nevertheless, it's still a very powerful marketing tool, as long as you use it well.

If you can strike up a conversation between your brand and your users it ceases to be just the products or services that sell a company, it's peer recommendations on digital communities. Thanks to social media even the smallest companies can now become highly regarded within a large community. Some companies are still playing catch up but there's no excuse for a new company. Social media should be part of your marketing strategy from day one.

That doesn't mean jumping on Twitter the moment your company is founded and chatting to anyone who'll listen. Social is a two-way medium and provides a great chance to research your clients, customers and competitors. Use social as part of a listening period, to find out how your potential audience interacts, how they discuss companies and even what your competitors are doing to 'befriend' them. It's never been quicker and cheaper to undertake detailed research before a product is even built, let alone launched.

One fundamental mistake companies make is to view Twitter as the 'fun side' of their business, as a separate entity to their marketing strategy. While it's fine to vary the nature of your messages across platforms, all communications - even tweets - should be part of that strategy. Your social media account shouldn't be opened until you've planned what you want to get from having it.

Some pitfalls seem to be made repeatedly and overkill is a major issue. If you start with all guns blazing, you might build up a quick following, but how are you going to keep that audience engaged? Do you have the resources to

keep up that pace of social media in month two, year two? If not then you're in danger of having a large following but no real connection, and of people leaving you. As they say in Texas: 'Big hat, no cattle!'

Companies often rush to start advertising on new platforms. While Facebook ads and promoted tweets can work, there is also the risk of alienating potential audiences. This form of marketing should only really be undertaken if there is a very specific, honed reason for it; for example a competition that is region specific and can be advertised just to that region. From a cost perspective I personally don't see the value, especially not to a small business as it is very difficult to gain a meaningful audience, let alone customers, from social media advertising.

The real skill in social marketing is to measure the right statistics. A lot of companies get het-up with their number of followers but, really, engagement and cut-through with your network is far more important than size. What percentage of your network clicks through from social media to your website? How many people are sharing or retweeting your communications? Are people you meet on networks even becoming customers? These are the meaningful stats that can be measured easily with

services such as Clout and Peer Index, and are definitely worth implementing into a wider strategy.

New social media platforms seem to launch every week, but that doesn't mean you should rush to sign up. Be wary about jumping on to the next big thing; you risk spreading yourself too thin. The move should only be made if your followers are already there, as your company's social profile needs to be led by your followers, not by trends.

The good news is that social media provides a way for small companies to compete with big business for audience attention. All the opportunities are there for a new company to reach the same amount of eyes as a multi-national, but only if you have rich, relevant content that is rolled out as part of a larger, thought-out strategy.

Mastering Your Market

Nicolas Carey
Take Note! Student Advertising

Take Note! offers an innovative and young mix of media to bridge the gap between businesses and students

The chances are you know a lot about your field. Problem is, your competitors probably know a lot about it too and so how are you supposed to become the go-to company?

For me, understanding the market place has been central to enjoying my time as an entrepreneur. It's also been the cornerstone of any success I've had. As a fledgling entrepreneur, it struck that I could make life much easier for myself if I chose a market I knew incredibly well.

I'd lived the student life for a while and understood how that market ticked, so tapping in to it seemed to be a quick way of becoming an authority in my field. At least that was the plan.

Considering you have to live and breathe a start-up business, focusing on a market you enjoy helps to maintain focus even when business gets tough. When I first started brainstorming the direction of my business, I found it pretty helpful to contemplate a couple of questions.

First, I needed to establish whether entering this market would make me any money because if the answer was no – what was the point? The easiest way to find out if there is money there is to check if there is already a competitor. It's a bit of a cliché, but if you think you have no competition, unless you're a genius, it's nearly always because there is no money in what you are getting into.

I then had to be honest about how excited I was about the market. If you're going to be doing this every day for the next god knows how long, you want to be passionate about your market, otherwise how will you have the drive to beat your competitors? Being passionate goes a long way towards helping you innovate in that market.

The next stage was to ask myself whether I could still relate to that market. If I couldn't even relate to the audience, then communicating with them would have been tricky, and appealing to them near impossible. This is especially true in the age of social media as how will you make them 'lol' and like your brand if you can't post up the perfect .jpg? Brands come to our company because we're youth-orientated and that helps us relate to our audience as well as building trust – the foundations of a solid business.

So having identified the youth market as my potential field of excellence, I quickly realised I didn't have any experience. Despite my mammoth ambition I was, in fact, a fresh-faced, 22-year-old just out of university and struggling to gain credibility with multinational clients. Trust me, it was an uphill challenge, but I learnt a few tricks to prove to the world just how much I knew.

The first was to track changes in my audience's habits and be the first to new trends. We researched trends among 18-21 year olds and then produced a report to pinpoint mistakes that companies made when trying to reach students. We utilised this to highlight how we could tap into market better than anyone else, and guess what? Clients were interested.

We then began to publish research to blogs or guest-post on sites to help Take Note reach the top of relevant Google searches. Guest posting within a credible channel also helped us to demonstrate our knowledge of the market and gain a bit of a voice.

From there we looked to build a personal profile around our market, in order to become an opinion maker. Speaking at events and entering competitions has been a great platform for getting noticed and made us lots of connections, some of which have become new business.

—

Mind you, we've been doing all this in the three years since we started, but it's only now that we're seeing the rewards

—

Having patience has become my final lesson. Despite planting the seeds for success through research, case studies and reports, the hardest thing is that there is a sizeable amount of time between doing that and people actually recognizing you as a go-to company in your market.

But it's been exciting. We're really making headway and becoming known as a leader in what we do. Of course, now we've started to nail it, I'm beginning to wonder what else I might know and how can I do it all over again in a new market.

Embrace the Social Video Clutter

Rory Ahern
Rubber Republic

There's a good chance that you've already seen a piece of Rubber's work, likely in an email marked YOU HAVE TO WATCH THIS! Their web videos Bodyform Responds and Vango Space Camping went viral last year, clocking millions of views in just a few months.

The creative services industry is going through something of a renaissance period experiencing an unprecedented era of change which I'm not sure even the industrial revolution could match for sheer speed.

In 2001 nobody knew what broadband was but in 2013 YouTube is getting one billion views a month. That's quite a leap!

At its heart, anyone's job in the creative industry has remained pretty much the same - to continually look at a blank piece of paper and ask what you could do with it. The difference from, say, 20 years ago is that there are a lot more things you can turn it into, viral video being one of them.

Five years ago, businesses didn't want to take viral videos seriously. It's a big challenge for them. Generally their brand and their marketing teams have been trained to regurgitate their brand doctrine over and over again. In a social world they had to a little brave and let go of what they wanted to say the whole time. Funnily enough most audiences don't want to sit on the end of a funnel for brand advertising. In this new connected world, brands need quality content that people will hunt for and which rewards them for sharing it, whether that is in cultural currency or yet more content.

It has been a long process for brands to understand this and realise that they can no longer just push bland branded messages to their audience. For those companies which have embraced this wholeheartedly and produced really good quality content, audiences now will actively hunt out branded content; even share it with their friends to look on-trend. The content might not reflect the product (what do extreme sports have to do with a Red Bull sticky drink for instance?) but the logo is pasted all over it and reinforce the name over and over again.

As an advertiser, in 2008, I was attracted to creative content but it was becoming clear that there were boundless possibilities on the horizon; possibilities which never could have been achieved through traditional advertising channels. You can now reach millions of

people with niche content on a very modest budget. And not only will people watch it but also share it, comment on it, give you feedback and perhaps even apply their own spin - extending the content's lifespan even further.

However, as someone turning 40 a scary realisation soon dawned that young creatives were probably better qualified than me in this area. While there used to be a strict hierarchical way of climbing through an ad agency, now we are having to fast track these young creatives as they are completely immersed and plugged in to this online world. They should become any good agency's cultural antenna. If you are a young person now, likelihood is that you are already part of numerous social networks where sharing, researching, creating and connecting is everyday practice. Well that actually makes you extremely well prepared for the modern creative industries.

What I have noticed is that, within modern social networks, if you are willing to continually make things, you will soon build a community from your efforts.

The tools for digital creation are so simple these days that you can try every idea you have and gain attention as you do. I think that is doubly important for a new agency because, nowadays, you can build an audience that will

quite literally follow you throughout your entire career; and that is an incredibly powerful asset to have when approaching potential clients.

But while it's never been easier to publish content to millions, be it through Tumblr or YouTube or Twitter, it's probably never been harder to gain attention due to there being so much content available. Our job is to find a way of making people click on a piece of branded content – which they generally don't want to do – instead of the latest K-pop dance craze or screaming goats. We also have to be very aware of the anti-advertising atmosphere on social networks and first be able to answer 'what permission does this brand have to invade an audience's space?' It's a sensitive balance and can be a real turn off when companies jump aboard audience-created trends.

So engaging a mass audience is a tough ask, but with the right angles it can be huge and there are no agencie's or individuals better positioned to take advantage than young, upcoming ones.

Making Your Own Success

Jim Orkney
Kinneir DuFort

Kinneir Dufort has been innovating everyday
products since the late seventies, including their 1984
Technophone - effectively the first ever pocket sized
mobile phone!

Strong ideas are the backbone of any client-based creative company.

Usually, money-making ones are generated in response to
a client brief, but creative people have ideas all the time,
they don't just switch on the 'ideas tap' when a brief drops
into the inbox. Back in 1988 we were a five person team
with no design awards and a rather modest profile, but,
we had initiative, talent and a strong urge to improve our
position – and quickly. So we examined how we could use
our latent, idea-generating talents to fast-track building
an impressive client portfolio.

Our answer was to turn the tables. Rather than wait for
clients to issue us with a brief for the things they wanted,
we'd identify potential briefs to deliver things that clients
didn't yet know they needed.

One of our most important starting points was reading
the business section of newspapers and seeking out
articles on companies that, typically, had developed a new
product or piece of technology which we thought held the
prospect of a design brief – in other words an opportunity
we could create a project for.

One week the team read a story about Radio Data System
(RDS); a new radio technology developed by the BBC that
was capable of delivering useful programme information
alongside the broadcast itself (the station name,
broadcast frequency etc.). Reading the report, which was
rather technical, it was clear that here was a technology
with nothing to excite a consumer's imagination. The
technology was great for engineers, but it did not engage
or affect the consumer at all.   This was a Eureka moment;
the realisation that we could take the initiative, go to the
BBC, and persuade them that we should design a new
consumer radio to help promote RDS.

Of course it wasn't quite that simple. The BBC didn't
know that they needed any help and we had to work out
who to persuade. The engineer quoted in the newspaper
was our first port of call and, while interested to hear
from us, he didn't have the experience, authority or
budget to commission a design project. To add to our
disappointment he didn't know anyone at the BBC who'd
ever done such a thing either! Despite these drawbacks,
after weeks of telephone calls we found our way up the
BBC's management tree and I was granted a meeting with
the then director of BBC Enterprises.

This was a first. A pitch where the 'client' wasn't aware
that they even needed a design intervention, who had
never commissioned such assistance and who had no
design brief other than the one I had drafted myself. It was
not a very promising start!

However, as the meeting unfolded my hopes rose. The
Director of Enterprises seemed to become intrigued with
the idea of designing a domestic radio to demonstrate
RDS technology: 'how long would it take?', 'what would it
all cost?', 'when could we start?' It was beginning to look
like it could happen.

Sure enough, within a matter of weeks we had our first
purchase order to design the 'radio of the future'. This was
to be our first project with a big name, prestige client and,
significantly, it was all entirely of our own making.

The benefits of this pro-active approach extended far
beyond payments from the project itself because the
BBC, having commissioned the design and prototype
model from us, duly went on to heavily publicise the new
radio as a way to trumpet their own RDS technology.
The BBC's promotional campaign caught the attention
of newspapers, which in turn helped us to get the story
into design journals both in the UK and abroad. Design
Week particularly liked it and for the first time Kinneir
Dufort was front page; headline material with a profile
as a pioneering design consultancy that, in the words of
Design Week "looked beyond the horizons of marketing".

We learned a lot from this experience; mainly that through
being being pro-active and persuasive it is possible to
generate new design business entirely by the power of
suggestion. In creating a project this way – literally taken
from newspaper article to inspiration to product – we also
learnt that aspiring to generate exciting and innovative
design results, with a powerful partner, can quickly build
reputation and help win new business.

These learnings may seem obvious, and many others have
no doubt done it better. Nevertheless, we certainly have
benefited from taking this approach over the years and
have come to recognise that when it comes to success,
a creative sales and marketing initiative is equally as
important as any great design.

Team WORK makes THE Dream WORK

Building a Team from Scratch

Ben Trewhella
Opposable Games

Born out the Bristol Games Jam, the Opposable team have gone on to produce some of the most creative mobile games available today; not least the uniquely named 'Monsieur Baguette presents RNA transcription of Saccharomyces Cerevisiae'.

Amazing products are built by great teams; but how do you build a great team? The A-Team were thrown together after a crime they didn't commit, while the Fantastic Four were united by inconvenient mutations in space.

But those aren't models we can easily replicate – or want to. They do, however, highlight a common, important trait in any team and that's trust. The essence of any good team is a good spread of compatible skills and an ability to trust the work of the others. But how do you build trust?

The vision of founding Opposable Games started when I left a service agency with the ambition to create my own products. The problem was, producing a good video game takes a variety of highly specialised skills and so you basically have two options: join a great team or build one from scratch.

Having had the experience of doing both, I knew the more fulfilling journey was to build a team myself and so I began to research who was out there. At the time, Bristol was about to host its own Games Jam; an event where teams of artists, developers and coders are thrown together to create a computer game in 48 hours. It was a perfect opportunity to meet and work with new talent. So I invited a few select people to take part with me. After a frantic weekend, our team of once strangers had not only created a game but had witnessed how each other worked in a pressurised situation. We walked away with the seeds of a whole new company.

Received wisdom would suggest two people is a good number to start a business - as they can bounce ideas off each other. But as games development needs a number of very specialised skills, starting as a pair is impossible unless you employ straight away - and that takes money.

After the Games Jam we got together over a Chinese and agreed that all the skills required for a new games company were sat around the table. It made complete sense to me. I knew and respected these people's talent and realised that if I started on my own I'd end up employing them anyway. Games Jam had allowed everyone to see what each other was capable of and they liked what they saw. We had already built trust in the team and we hadn't even started a company. The question wasn't if we should work together, but how?

We had a chance to access primer funding, but we did not want to lose creative control or company direction by taking on investment. The answer was to found Opposable Games as a partnership of directors, where all employees had a share in the business, which would keep us all motivated and loyal to its success. But we needed to keep costs down.

To keep the company lean we decided that all of our directors would continue their freelance activities. It meant that everybody was still going out, networking and innovating outside of Opposable but that we could then jump on opportunities as Opposable when they arose. The added bonus to that model is that when there aren't any interesting projects on the horizon we, as Opposable, have no overheads, so we aren't forced to take on dull or uncreative projects to cover a salary bill – we can simply split off and do our own thing. It also means that when we do all come together people are excited and ready to get their head down; it avoids burn out.

—

Received wisdom would suggest two people is a good number to start a business - as they can bounce ideas off each other

—

It wasn't all plain sailing though, and this model isn't for the faint-hearted. Managing the range of emotions across six new directors is a test. While other companies often hire staff on the strength of short interviews, offering shares to a group of relative of strangers could have been a major gamble. However, the highly pressurised nature of the Games Jam allowed me to quickly see who could and who couldn't handle it, in a way sifting through 50 CVs and interviewing for 20 minutes would never have done. The key lesson was to make sure you really do know who you're getting involved with and what their talents really are.

Nonetheless, I do think that with the employment market moving the way it is, we will start to see more young creatives begin to found companies which are flexible, born out of collaboration and with a literal shared interest. In the games industry so many big companies are in real trouble because work is drying up yet they still have huge overheads to handle. Thanks to technological advances, one person can now do the work of three or four and so perhaps more of these smaller groups - who can come together, create something and then disband - will fill the void.

Turning Friends into a Business Team

B.U.S.I

Alex Ryley
Mutant Labs

After starting out of university, the Mutant team quickly developed a name for themselves while producing games and apps for clients including Moshi Monsters and Absolute Radio.

During our final year of university a few friends and I had the idea of starting a company. Given the lack of jobs in the real world, it seemed like a good idea. But it immediately raised the question – is setting up with your friends such a good idea?

At the end of university most graduates tend to go off in their own direction and the groups they've been working with over the past three years just disband. We thought that was crazy, and wanted to see if we could keep our group together.

There were apprehensions, of course. The whole idea of starting a company was unnerving given that none of us had any previous business experience. It seemed like a huge obstacle to overcome. However, we soon learned to do things bit-by-bit. It's a gradual process and with every week you gain experience and become that little bit more familiar with the ins-and-outs of running a company. The only decision we felt completely sure about was working together. We'd hear that starting a company with friends can have many pitfalls, especially as there were five of us and all recent graduates. But, we were confident we could overcome them, and to ensure any future problems would be minimised we took the precaution of a well-drafted shareholders agreement. Having standards and rules outlined in writing from day one was a worthwhile investment. You might start out as friends with the best intentions, but things can happen in business - what if somebody leaves? what if somebody isn't pulling their weight? - and if you have signed agreements for reference then so many complicated issues can be avoided.

Personally, we didn't see the risk of falling out with each other as any greater than any other business partners falling out - friends or not. We were getting on well at the time and were confident our relationship was strong enough to take the gamble.

It didn't take long to discover that the benefits of working with your friends far outweigh the risks. For one, the feeling of being in it together makes starting the company exciting, and less frightening. We were lso more likely to be on the same page when decisions had to be made and were able to start out with a shared vision that we each understood.

One thing we had to be conscious about was taking the business seriously and not allowing our friendships to detract from that. Thankfully it wasn't difficult, once you are signing lengthy legal documents you quickly realise that starting a company is a serious undertaking. A lot of people worry about their work/life balance and that starting up with friends might blur those lines.

A potential recipe for disaster was that, in the beginning, the five of us all shared a house. We worked and lived together, not quite what they mean by work/life balance, but actually it was good fun. As a group we always enjoyed jamming ideas, so being able to carry that on at home suited our style. Living together made office space very important though, as working from home doesn't provide any natural separation - and long-term can damage your productivity. With an office we could leave business in the workplace and the daily commute became a transition between mind sets.

There was a question of deciding who does what - which side of the business each of us needed to handle. None of us had any experience in director positions and so we just had to look at our existing personalities and figure out who would be best placed at what. The only time that ever caused issues was when roles began to overlap. The solution came back to having our roles clearly defined from the outset. Happily, we've also ended up with a democracy of five and so while we might not always agree there's always a majority!

It all depends on the dynamic within your friendship group. We were fine working and living together in the early days but that might not be right for everybody. The key thing that we've learnt is to separate business and friendship in our heads and not take issues home – which of course is easier said than done. Maybe the way we've done it is quite unorthodox. But so far it seems to be working out well for us.

Hiring Your First Employee

Rad Dougall
Studioworks

The classic tale of a company emerging from an over-busy freelancer, Studioworks now has an office brimming with digital talent and clients across the country.

When you're the only person working in your business, it's really tough knowing when it's the right moment to hire someone else.

After a year of being the sole employee at Studioworks, I found myself working 12 hour days and eating too many ready meals. While I enjoyed having creative control over every project, I knew that I could no longer keep up with demand.

I was also getting to a point where potential clients were beginning to judge me on size. The viewpoint that I couldn't get the job done because I wasn't big enough (not like that, calm down) was very frustrating - and in my opinion a load of nonsense. Nevertheless, those views weren't going to change and so I'd reached the stage where I needed some help.

Despite the pressure, hiring someone was still a big decision. Could I afford the salary? Would they drain away my profit margin? What happened if the extra capacity didn't generate new contracts? Could I afford to pay someone year-on-year, as well as myself?

I wanted assurance so I wrote out some calculations based on potential new work vs increased costs, but, to be honest; at that stage it was still speculative. It was about belief and taking a bit of a punt. I had to ask myself what I wanted. I set up a company to build a business. I didn't set it up just to do nice work or flatter my own ego. I wanted the business to make money. My big fear was becoming the company's bottleneck. So I reckoned, long-term, I needed staff who could deliver the work, eventually, without me altogether.Decision made!

I got someone in to help me with employment contracts. This was absolutely crucial, not least because the laws are so complicated these days and it's very easy get into hot water. I'm so glad that I spent the £300 on a decent HR consultant as it's probably saved me a fortune in the long run.

The critical factor, of course, was being able to find the right person. I used all the free channels I could like social media, universities and local industry group Meetdraw. I'd taken the decision early on not to spend what little resources I had on employment agencies, they are useful but not cost effective when you're just starting up.

I ended up with around 35 applications but, with it being my first appointment, I felt compelled to interview every single candidate. Despite being time consuming, this actually turned out to be a great

Ian, as I found a second contender who I would have written off based on his CV.

So this gave me two winners but a real dilemma in choosing one for the position. They had different strengths, different experience and different education. In almost every way they were opposites. When I said I was taking a bit of a punt, I actually super-sized myself to go double or quits! Much to my own surprise I employed both of them. Now that was scary, but I just couldn't pass up on the opportunity and thankfully they have both won me work which, as a sole trader, I could never have contemplated.

Since then I have hired another six staff and as a rule only employ people who are smarter than me. Some business owners struggle with this concept, but you won't get anywhere by wanting to know more than everyone else on your team.

Being a young boss can be a difficult balance at times. Although I want to be a friend to my team, I have to constantly remind myself that I won't always get invited to the pub because, no matter what, I'm the 'big scary boss'. In fact this is a good thing; you shouldn't set up a business to make friends, it's there to make money, and there are times when you might have to make difficult decisions about staff to support that goal. If you're best mates, that can cloud your judgement.

Despite that, and at the risk of sounding mushy, as soon as I hire someone I want to look out for them, not just because I want to hang on to them but because I want them to love their job. I think that comes from having worked for some idiots in the past and being determined not to make Studioworks one of those places. I'm always trying to improve working conditions, benefits, surroundings, fun, happiness, flexibility and these are things that mostly cost nothing but can mean a lot.

All this sounds like a grand plan but, really, I just give my team the tools to do their job effectively and let them get on with it. At first that was a terrifying prospect, but in time it's paid to let go, recruit well and have trust in my staff. It's freed up a lot of my time to run the business and stopped me being the bottleneck in the operation.

Investing in New Talent

Bob Mytton
Mytton Williams

D&AD Award winners Mytton Williams look every inch a London outfit but, with their focus on 'no fluff', are in fact a proud South West agency with clients including Waitrose, the Royal Photographic Society and The National Trust .

When do people start to become talented?

Mozart was 21 when he composed his first piano masterpiece, Mark Zuckerburg built Facebook at university and Mary Shelley had completed Frankenstein by her 20th birthday. So why do employers sometimes seem so worried about hiring young graduates?

In the mid-nineties I taught one day a week at Bath Spa University and got to meet some fantastic young designers. It may have left me biased, but when I started Mytton Williams I didn't think twice about hiring a new graduate as our first employee, in fact the first few employees had all recently graduated. While there was an aspect of 'giving back' by employing them, they certainly brought some benefits of their own.

One huge upside is the fresh approach they bring to projects. There is no 'this is the way we do things' attitude, no learnt methods. Having that 'can-do' mindset in the company instantly brought a new approach to the work.

Although Mytton Williams has been trading for 17 years, we still take on recent graduates for pretty much the same reason. A young employee tends to be more in touch with current, what people like and how people are starting to work. I've been in the industry for 25 years and so perhaps am less in touch with creative trends. These youngsters haven't been through the system, they're not constrained by the learnings of one particular design company and this means they can spot new ways around a project that an entrenched veteran probably wouldn't.

There are, of course, risks when bringing young talent in to your company. Their lack of experience can show through in how they interact with older clients, which can be a little uncomfortable, and it can also show in the standard of their artwork. However, for

me, the benefits of hiring someone at the very start of their career far outweigh the risks. Young employees are a cost-effective way of expanding your team and your work load, especially if money is tight. Not only is it cheaper to hire a graduate but at the start of their career they are also very enthusiastic. In the early years, having that enthusiasm in the office was perfect because, as new business owners, we were hungry to make a success of everything that came through the door. We were working very hard to grow our business and the recent graduates were working equally as hard to prove themselves as designers; our ambitions matched.

Generally I've found that the better graduates stay for two or three years and then leave for London. The fact that younger talents are more likely to leave might be an issue for some agencies, but I don't think it has to be a problem. Being forced to replace a graduate after a few years just means another set of those fresh eyes coming in, and that can make up for any retraining.

Oddly, people only ever ask about the risks of hiring younger, relatively un-established talent, not the pros; and they never ask about the risks of hiring older, more established creatives. The danger there is very often they are less in touch with the goings-on of digital and social – and frequently not interested to get involved with it either. Sometimes, after so many years in industry, they have a set of go-to methods and in today's world, if they're not changing, they're out of date. When that happens, existing ideas have to be challenged in order to avoid staleness – and bringing in youngsters is one way of keeping the whole office on their toes. The mix of old and new blood has always been good for our company.

I've been lucky to have forged relationships with young creatives through lecturing and maintaining links with education, but it's a relationship that any agency could, and probably should, be making. While, yes, it will have benefits for your agency, above all, the creatives graduating now are the future of this industry and it's imperative that we help develop them.

The Benefits of Collaboration

Ben Risk

Before founding interdisciplinary creative network Forge Munroe, Ben was the former head of business development at 422 South and a regarded artist and gallery owner in his own right.

There is only so much you can achieve alone, only so many hours in the day, only so many skills one person can have, and there are times when you want to be able to do so much more.

An obvious solution is to collaborate with other people, but it's not a path everyone is sold on. Personally, I have to ask: what sort of person would rather work on their own when there is constant opportunity to be amazed by someone else? But I'm a serial collaborator so that's the sort of thing I would say!

Collaboration has probably been the most important aspect of my career. When you set your mind on an ambitious project, working with other designers, directors, animators, writers, in fact agencies of all sorts gives you the power to be that little bit more ambitious; and you can never have enough expertise in your back pocket as far as I'm concerned.

When I first entertained the idea of collaborating it gave me a sense that I was more adaptable. Freelancers are all too aware that pooling skills is a smart way to deliver more ambitious projects but it's an approach companies can gain a lot from too. When you work with an interesting partner, ideas flow and that can lead to projects which you hadn't even envisaged. In this way collaborating has not just been important, it has also been enjoyable – and inspiring.

I've found the right collaborations have been a great vehicle for getting noticed, especially if you work with a larger company. It's a fast track to get your name on to new clients' radars. They may be keeping tabs on a larger company but once they've seen you're co-working, you pop onto the radar too.

Size shouldn't be an issue either – if the idea is strong it's always worth a punt. There have been times where I've had an idea I couldn't possibly have achieved by myself, so I've sought out the biggest, boldest collaborator I could think of, who was right for the project at least. It's surprising that even if they don't know you from Adam, there's usually a friendly voice on the other end of the phone and if you've the right idea, who knows what's possible.

By working with others, I feel like I've doubled my time in the industry. The shared experience is incredible, and why would you choose to learn from your mistakes when you could learn from someone else's? Collaborating has also

roved great for contacts. Many times I've been able to pull these networks of past collaborators and found myself the centre of a knowledge web. That is a very powerful source to have access to.

owever, simply engineering collaboration will not arantee its success. There are many potential pitfalls orking with others and how relationships are managed n make or break a project.

—

By working with others, I feel like I've doubled my time in the industry

—

eing up front about finances at the start of a project n help avoid any awkward situations. I'm also quite lective about who I work with. Keeping a small number ` tight knit collaborators has been a better model than ying to collaborate with the world, just in terms of trust d security.

Non-disclosure agreements are always important if it's your own concepts or IP that will be worked on, as you hear nightmare stories about ideas and clients being stolen. You need to build trust and probably a strong friendship before embarking on a joint project. It all comes back to picking the right partnerships.

Overall it's proved a very rewarding experience. What's more it has never been easier to find interesting people to work with. I often just use the internet to find the creator of a piece of work I like – but going out and meeting these people, getting to know them is certainly the best way. You have to be able to meet someone and see possibilities where others might not, to look in unusual places as well as at conferences and festivals. The internet is great but it is difficult to build strong relationships over a keyboard. It may seem like all the creative collaborations are happening on Twitter but, really, get down to somewhere like the Breakfast Club in East London and you'll overhear a hundred project ideas. If you can then make yourself a part of that conversation who knows where interesting new friendships might lead!

Sole Traders Don't Have to Work Alone

Debbie Rawlings
Auroch Digital

Leading games studio Auroch has recently masterminded Bristol's first ever games hub, a community business space in which games companies can work, interact and collaborate.

In an increasingly digitised world, there are very few jobs which can be done alone. Whether you're an artist, developer, even a project manager you have to work with other people to deliver anything.

The odd thing about this is that the creative sector has one of the highest numbers of freelancers and sole traders of any industry. However, all of these people need to work with others before any product can be built or any project delivered to a client. Seeing that the world is digital, all of this work can be simply bounced from person to person via email and Dropbox. Thousands of people working in bedroom offices, kitchen tables and garden sheds emailing each other; It paints a lonely picture and it's not a lot of fun.

This is especially true in the games industry. Producing a game is a tricky process which demands different specialised skills at different stages of the project. While creativity is of course important, the project management of a game is critical. Creating an amazing product is no mean feat. For instance, Angry Birds was the developer's 52nd title and I'll give you one guess as to how successful the other 51 were.

This means that success is very hard for one person to achieve alone. You need the input of others but, with everyone working remotely or hot-desking, getting that type of meaningful interaction is difficult. This is why hubs are so important to the creative industries.

A hub provides a dedicated space, an infrastructure and a culture that allows fellow entrepreneurs to work co-operatively; sharing ideas, technology, skills, knowledge and experience. It doesn't work for everyone, but I've found that these types of communities are far more important to companies in the creative industries than in other sectors. I'm sure that if you asked the MD of a finance or insurance firm to share their business ideas and working methods with supposed competitors, they would probably laugh you out of the building! In our industry, however, technology and trends change so quickly that learning from each other is the norm and can provide a distinct advantage for everyone involved.

While having companies share ideas may appear mad, success in the creative industries is as much about your relationships within the 'scene' as it is about talent. The games industry is such a monstrous global platform with thousands of competitors and millions of potential clients, that at a local level, creative companies have much more to gain from cooperation. That isn't to say everything in a hub is fair game. As creators we respect each other's work and have a mutual understanding that if something isn't public, what you see in the hub stays in the hub.

Another advantage we find when working in a hub is the access to new talent. When you're working on new project you need different resources at different stages. If you're then surrounded by skilled and talented people it makes it much easier to meet potential collaborators, discover others you might want to work with and find out if they're available – all over a chat in the kitchen. Essentially it cuts down waiting time and recruitment costs.

Before you plunge into a shared working space, though, it's worth checking that it has flexible terms. When we're creating games we scale up quickly for projects and scale down again. We've negotiated to hire desk space on a month to month basis, so that if/when we scale back down again, we don't have to keep shelling out for desks we're not using.

Perhaps the surprising aspect of it all is the confidence being part of a hub gives the company. As well as physical benefits, being part of an established creative hub helped put us on the map. For instance our shared space is the go-to spot for journalists looking for quotes, and the first place an industry bod might consider for a product launch. More excitingly, when one of our fellow companies make it big, or create a product with a big buzz, we all share in that celebration. And it gives us all a little spotlight by proxy!

Of course you can do it all by yourself – and there are plenty of successful agencies who do – but really, where's the fun in that?

Being Thrifty isn't the Same as Being Cheap

Vicky Brophy
Wonky Films

WONKY work as a collective of creatives; combining
illustrators, animators, musicians and writers to create
animated content for clients such as Adidas, Radio One
and The British Heart Foundation.

Alongside death and taxes, the only other certainty in business is that starting a company costs money. Just how much, however, depends on the type of operation you're willing to run.

My partner and I have always known that we didn't want Wonky to be owned by anyone else, or have to worry about repaying loans, and so we started out with pretty much whatever was in our pockets. It meant we've had to be highly thrifty. Thrifty is a confusing word – it doesn't mean cheap, it means being careful with your money. If you're cheap the chances are that you'll end up making some false economies which will bite you on the backside later on.

There are plenty of luxuries you can do without in the early days, for instance a studio or office. We found that a coffee shop with Wi-Fi was perfect, up until we started generating enough income to justify renting our first space. The problem was, it wasn't just rent that comes with a studio; it's insurance, business rates, heating, electricity, line rental, internet… loo roll. Boy, does it get expensive!

Strange as it may sound, another in the 'nice-to-have' category was permanent staff. Although they cost more per day, employing freelancers allows you the flexibility of cutting them loose during the leaner times. We also lecture at local universities to spot upcoming talent, so can offer them work experience placements to test them out on internal projects and then possibly smaller client briefs. Schemes like that are mutually beneficial, they get invaluable industry experience and we dramatically cut our costs.

While we were able to cut some corners initially, those nice-to-haves soon become must-haves. One moment we were fine and then we'd check our cash flow and get a shock. It taught us not to spend everything that was available and to keep a cash float for unexpected problems. At the same time, we never put off paying for things like insurance, security and legal advice as we knew they would save us money in the long term.

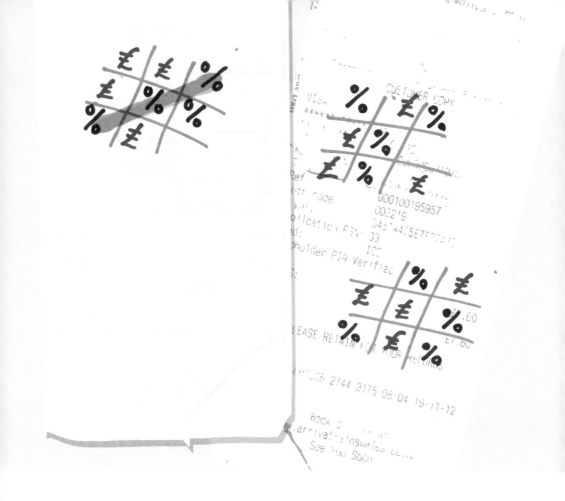

...e found that out when somebody nipped into our ...stairs window and stole our computer – at least we had ...ntents insurance but we still had to pay the excess! It ...t only became much harder to find an insurer but it ...o got more expensive. Something as simple as buying ...ndow locks would have saved us a fortune! We've also ...und legal advice particularly handy for getting solid but ...xible contracts in place. The other option, which can be ...re cost-effective, is to get standard industry contracts ...joining member organisations such as PACT.

—

Where we really struck gold was discovering all the things you can get for nothing

—

...other great place to save money long term is in ...e accounts. By having a good accountant who ...derstands our position we've saved much more money ...an we've ever paid her - on things like tax savings and ...t rate VAT schemes. To keep costs down even more ...also opted to undertake the book keeping ourselves,

just by using a simple spreadsheet – no fancy software required! As well as sparing us a few quid it meant that we were fully on top of our spending and understood every penny that came in and out.

Where we really struck gold was discovering all the things you can get for nothing. We were surprised by how many things really are free if you look in the right places, like funded learning schemes, competitions and grants through the likes of Skillset, Business Link or Creative England. I even managed to wing free trips to China, Mexico, France and Holland in the space of 12 months. Networking at free events and contributing to conferences can lead to all kinds of opportunities, trust me. We networked our way into Number 10 by year two and even bagged a new client in the Cabinet Room!

There have been some obvious basics that we've kicked ourselves for forgetting, occasionally. Experience has taught us to always set a fee with partners or freelancers once you do win that client as, weirdly, people tend to take longer than initially anticipated when you're paying by the day. Who'd have thought!

Making Cash Flow

Roger Proctor
Proctor and Stevenson

As distinguished CVs go, few in the creative
industries will rival that of Roger Proctor;
MD of Proctor & Stevenson, Fellow of the
Royal Society of Arts and Member of the
British Empire to boot.

There is an old adage that 'cash is king'. In the age of credit it may seem an anachronism but now, more than ever, it is true.

Despite it forever being on everyone's list of business problems, mine included, cash flow is only really your ability to manage the amount of money coming in against the amount being paid out. Understanding that simple truth, then measuring and managing cash flow is how we learn to live with it.

At times we all want to hide under the sheets and ignore our cash flow, but doing so can sink even the sturdiest company. There are plenty of stories where a company's business has been good, delivering projects to very happy clients, but because they haven't been sending out or chasing up invoices on time, they have gone bust. On paper they may have been profitable but their bank was not prepared to extend a loan. While you might trust your clients, the bank probably won't.

Unfortunately for most creative people, there is a tendency to see the whole area of cash flow as secondary to actual work and, quite frankly, boring headache. However, managing cash flow is far less of a pain than ceasing to trade. As a way of running from the issue, many are tempted by factoring. Factoring is where a bank will pay you a percentage of the invoice and charge you high interest until they are paid by your client. I have so often seen businesses go down this road and for it all to end in bankruptcy. This has often been because the reason clients aren't paying is because they aren't really happy, and having a bank in to factor your invoices probably isn't going to change that!

So there are some very simple principles to observe regarding cash flow. To start with, at the beginning of a project make it a condition with the client that you will bill on a monthly and intermediate basis whatever the stage of the project. They should accept this principle as it is common practice and if they don't, be suspicious.

It may seem obvious, but I have always fixed payment terms at 30 days. This is perfectly normal and I make it a priority to have those terms bold and upfront on each and every client invoice. If a client doesn't pay on time I've always found it best to contact them straight away. Ask them if there is a problem as it is better to know than not, especially if they are likely to default on you.

One piece of information I have always kept to hand is when the last day a client's accounts payable team will accept an invoice. That way

u can make sure you always beat that submission date. Until you
st a client, ideally after a long trading history together, it's best not
get sucked in to being asked by your client to pay suppliers on their
half because 'their paperwork is too difficult' to expedite. I've found
at it will often come back to bite you.

ave also always tried to build up a reserve of at least three times
y monthly outgoings. That doesn't mean cash in the bank but a
culation on the difference on what you owe and what you are
ed, if everyone paid each other. So if your monthly overheads of
aries, cars and rent are £10,000, you should try and have a trading
rplus of £30,000 if you paid everyone and everyone paid you. While
nderstand this might be very difficult for some, it is also very
rthwhile, especially if someone goes bust on you. In that respect,
en your agency does have a good month try not to go out on a
ending spree. Always remember things can go up as well as down,
d cash in the bank is a safety net that should remove a weight from
ur shoulders.

—

At times we all want to hide under the sheets and ignore our cash flow, but doing so can sink even the sturdiest company

—

nally, the key to many of my dealings has simply been to build good
d open relationships with suppliers. It shouldn't amaze you to know
at if you build goodwill by paying them promptly, then if you're
ving a cash flow problem, they may well support you with temporary
edit. You'll be surprised how accommodating other companies can
towards a valued customer!

When to Reinvest Early Profits

Tom Frost
Crack Magazine

Despite launching in just 2009, Crack has expanded rapidly across the UK, enjoying cross promotions with the likes of Nike and kick-starting street press publishing along the way.

Starting out there was never any plan about what we'd do if we made some money. In the publishing industry it's almost a bit of a novelty to make any at all.

For us, the nature of cash flow and invoicing means that money comes and goes in dribs and drabs. Seeing as we haven't landed that massive pay load which means we can just run off and be rich, it's meant we've learnt to reinvest little pockets into the company when we can.

There are so many outgoings in our business that our attitude to profit is always 'caution'. Wages, print run, rent, bills, travel – there are so many possibilities for unseen costs that we've found it useful to play it safe and leave a little bit in the bank. That means if, say, a VAT bill comes in higher than expected, you're still going to be covered. Living in the times we do, with costs spiralling at a moment's notice, that just seems like basic, common sense. Dull as it is, being thrifty with your cash and keeping some of it back for a surprise means that you'll never get into trouble.

But once you've got your bases covered, you can start to ask more interesting questions about what to do with profits. The most important question to ask first is: do you know where you're going? Largely for us, issue-to-issue it has been a case of constant reinvestment, of using any spare cash to drive growth. When Crack started it was quite a Bristol-centric magazine but the plan was always to branch out as widely as possible, and that meant investing in increased print runs. That was part of us looking at the long game. We could have remained comfortable as a Bristol-only magazine but we're ambitious people and so we expanded whenever it was possible.

It's important to keep control though. Using your cash to reinvest this way creates a danger of stretching too fast beyond your means and being unable to keep up with the demands made on the business. With Crack worried about expanding to a new city but no returning enough advertising revenue to cove the extended run.

Every business move comes down to taking well-calculated risks though, being cautious over every aspect that could go wrong and eventually making the right call. That's easie said than done and we've definitely always had that sense of anticipation when expandi in to a new city, but we've yet to have a duff one. Like any company, contemplating a new product or a new market comes down to thorough risk assessment.

Still, it'll be a weird day when we're no longer investing our profits in to expansion. Part of n thinks we'll never stop, there are always new cities to reach and it's not as if we want the competition catching up with us. As much as anything, reinvesting profits is exciting; growi your business is exciting - meeting new peop making the product bigger and better. Withou constant reinvestment we'd have never growr or reinforced our brand, and if we hadn't don that then there's no way we'd have worked wi the profile of brands in the way we are today. We just did a fashion shoot with Nike and that generates content for the site. Even if thi does all sound a bit motivational speaking, I honestly think we might get bored if we're no reinvesting and growing.

I realise this isn't for everyone. There are pler of people running good businesses, growing at a steady pace and spending their profits on nice holidays. Hopefully there'll be a poin in the future when we can sit back and take a bit more money. But reinvestment has been essential in working with the bigger clients a gaining the bigger name that will allow us to get there. So be cautious with your gambles but do take them. This whole operation has been a risk, starting in the biggest downturn UK history has been a risk, but calculate whe to invest those little bits of cash you have an go for it.

Hiring a Financial Director

Steve Garratt
Giggle Group

Bristol-based Giggle Group specialise in film for broadcast and corporate clients alike, including JP Morgan, BBC, HSBC and twofour.

When I started, the world of account and tax profiles were as foreign to me as, well, a foreign country. Probably more foreign actually because you can take a holiday to foreign countries but you can't take a holiday to tax profile spreadsheets. Why would you?

In our early years we had a relatively short-term approach to finance and it was much more about clocking where we were rather than planning where we wanted to be. I had a finance manager in place, b she wasn't qualified and had simply learnt on the job under guidanc from our accountants, who we were very reliant on. While they had steered us through some storms I was fed up with the short-termism of how we were doing business. Whenever we started to build up a cash reserve I would get clobbered with something unexpected. Nothing was planned, we managed everything day-to-day, which is a very time consuming way of running a business. Boring as it sounds you need goals, targets and a strategy; something to aim for around which you can make the big decisions.

In 2012 two new directors invested in Giggle Group and that made me feel a real duty to get our finances in order. While we probably could have carried on as we were for another 10 years, at the end of i I suspect we'd have ended up with very little value in the business. W needed someone, but I had reservations about how much control a financial director might take from me. One of our key strengths at th point was taking decisive action when opportunities arose, and wou hiring an FD complicate that?

Still, I needed help and it was time for a change. We chose to hire a part-time FD and that came with its own concerns around integratio and communication. How could we help him to truly understand the business and our culture? Would we get the full value from him, wou he deliver and show a return on investment? The part-time hiring wa a compromise on those worries as Giggle Group was still pretty smal and I couldn't justify another full salary commitment at that point.

We had some clear goals for the FD, namely to stabilise the busines and ensure we had the correct systems to generate forecasting data. We also hoped an FD could help us analyse the jobs we undertook, determine which were making money and which weren't.

e've now had our FD for about a year and the biggest change has
een a cultural one. Numbers matter a lot more now, and we have
anagement accounts every month that are about half an inch thick!
ith all this data we can track trends, see the costs and then tweak
em here and there. In finance, nothing ever seems to happen quickly
d it will take a year to really see the effects on the bottom line, but I
n already feel the effects in the way we work.

—

**Whenever we started to build up a
cash reserve I would get clobbered
with something unexpected.
Nothing was planned, we managed
everything day-to-day, which is a very
time consuming way of running a
business**

—

hink that what I took away from the whole process was to spend your
me finding the right FD and be very clear about what you want them
do. If you don't have a plan how can you measure their success?
t keep it simple: improve profitability, increase gross margin by X%,
duce overheads – that sort of thing. They will tell you what's possible
d what isn't. We also discovered that it doesn't really matter if your
D is from outside of the creative sector. Numbers are numbers, gross
argin is always gross margin and profit is always what's left after
verything else has been paid. What matters is getting someone who
ts you rather than someone who's cool. Our FD wears a suit but he
wears a lot and gets the job done!

he biggest shock was realising that an FD isn't there to do all the
ork for you. In fact, you're likely to find yourself with more to do after
ring one because you probably weren't doing enough to start with!

Creative Business Funding

Pamela Peter-Agbia
Nom de Strip

An ale pub or Bristol nightclub might not be the place you'd expect to find a quality arts journal, but Nom de Strip's street press model is fast bringing the arts to unlikely places.

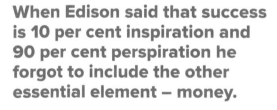

When Edison said that success is 10 per cent inspiration and 90 per cent perspiration he forgot to include the other essential element – money.

Having good ideas is common currency for many of us in the creative industries. Most of them come to nothing, but sometimes the idea to create something becomes so strong you're compelled to do something about it.

Any venture with a tangible product takes time and money to research, develop, build, market and sell; and being able to eat and live at the same time are nice luxuries worth preserving too!

Nom de Strip started out as a project between friends; we wanted to share and discuss interesting things happening in the South West arts in a publication. The project quickly built momentum, and as more people became aware of it, we realised the publication could actually be something more serious. Beyond friends and acquaintances, there was a much wider market interested in what we were doing but we lacked the money and resources to reach them.

We identified quite early on that any success would require the publication being a physically printed 'thing' that could be distributed to venues rather than a website, so printing was a significant cash outlay. Making the magazine is a labour of love, so we paid for a small print run of the first issue ourselves, and distributed them to as many venues as possible. The response from our peers and from the public was really positive and it gave us the confidence to keep going; to get bigger and better. However, to give the project life and realise its potential we needed funding and, to do that, we needed to turn what started out as a hobby into a viable business venture.

The arts sector is a funny part of the wider creative industry – it's not like film, gaming, or animation, with shoals of investors swimming around looking for the next big thing. Instead we're very fortunate to have funding bodies in this country who support artistic and cultural activity and so we approached the Arts Council.

Applying for funding is no breeze. It's not FREE money. It's a difficult, stressful process, which, to be honest, can take some of the energy and enthusiasm out of the project

self. On the plus side, it forces a level of introspection that probably wouldn't happen in any other circumstance.

pplying for funding gives you time to really consider nd understand every aspect of your organisation: what ou do, why you do it, how you do it and who for. I guess 's a similar process to applying for a bank loan, and no ank will lend you money unless they are 100% sure that ou have a successful business which will give a return n their investment. You have to think hard about what ou are applying for, how you want to invest that money nd how you will make it worthwhile for the people who re funding you. You also need to think about what you ill do if you don't get the money. Transferring a creative lea into a business application can be a real struggle and ompetition is tough. Only 40 per cent of Arts Council grant pplications are successful, so having a plan B is vital.

eeping your integrity is also important and we were orried about having obligations forced upon us from nders. There was also a concern that our partners might ave a slightly different agenda to ours, but it turned out nose worries were unfounded. The key thing is finding the ght people to invest in your project is if they believe in hat you're doing and don't want to change it too much. owever, you also have to accept that as a new venture,

working with new people, your project will change and develop anyway. It's natural. We now work in partnership with Peninsula Arts and Plymouth University and there is a mutual respect and vision for the publication built on honesty and transparency from both sides.

Building a company dependent on arts funding is always a gamble, as there is a real risk of the support disappearing. While there are some projects and organisations out there which understandably rely completely on funding and couldn't run without it, it's not a model I'd recommend for the long term. The impact on a business having funding removed is usually catastrophic and so we've always considered a mixed-revenue approach as the ideal. It's given us the incentive to scale the business to a size where we could sustain ourselves if and when funding does evaporate.

Fortunately, the Arts Council encourages this and requests that your bid be match-funded from the outset. Look to the people around you for lots of good advice and creative ideas on how to develop your own business model!

Love Can Fade - An Entrepreneur's Perspective on Investors

Ben Heald
Sift Media

Sift Media delivers original, branded content that is seen by over half a million professionals across the globe. In their 16 years, Sift has now gained five million page impressions, a figure most publishers would be jealous of!

There's something very seductive about venture capitalist investment. Ready money, no guarantees, no loan to pay off; and all you have to do in return is share your profits by handing over a reasonable stake of your company. At least that's what the brochure might say.

This is the story of a 12-year relationship I had with a London venture capital (VC) business when they invested £1.25m in Sift in 1999. As a CEO and business founder, the experience offers lessons which might be valuable to other budding entrepreneurs considering taking money from investors.

It may sound obvious, but names, funds and partners change. You do the deal with one set of people, but they can easily leave or be replaced. In my case, one of the initial investors was a fund that subsequently changed its manager (and thus my board member) twice, each with their own agendas and ambitions.

It is vital to cut deals right for the business, not those which impress the venture capitalists. For example, in November 2000, a month after our second round funding, we acquired CRM Forum Limited for approximately £500,000 and three per cent of Sift, but the day before we formally signed, we sat in a room and wondered if we should pull out of the deal. We felt it was wrong, but it was our first acquisition and, in our naivety, went ahead on the basis that we'd talked up the deal during the second round negotiations and wanted to impress. With more experience we'd have walked away.

Obviously taking investment means your stake will be diluted, but things get unbalanced when venture capitals have more than 50 per cent. It can encourage behaviour that is too fast and loose for a growing business. This can be exacerbated if VCs have invested at high values and your performance isn't stellar; they can take risks betting on achieving a much quicker return than is in any way realistic for the company's situation.

Depending on how desperate you are for investment, you may or may not be able to be fussy about who invests in the business. But don't forget to keep your investor under scrutiny. This means comparing stories with their other investees. Look up the carrying value of their investment in you and find out about the constitution of the fund; for instance who invested in it and what they were promised. Knowledge is power in all negotiation situations.

This also extends to VC representatives who sit on your board. They will have personal incentives and you need to understand what deal they have struck with the investment fund they represent. For example, they might just need to prove themselves by doing deals (any deal), but they might also have an incentive to exit by a fixed date. VCs are not like Angels. Your VC rep is not protecting and discussing his own money. He only cares about your business in the sense that he's playing a squash match he wants to win. On the other hand, as a founder you care because usually it's your money, and your life!

Investment should bring growth and the next challenge is to reinvent yourself as a CEO. The skills needed to found, grow and run a start-up are utterly different to those needed for a larger company and most founders can't make the transition. They generally get kicked out if the company misses a step, particularly if by then they've lost equity control. The reality is that founder-thinking can easily kill a growing business and if you want to stay involved, you've got to reinvent yourself.

—

It may sound obvious, but names, funds and partners change. You do the deal with one set of people, but they can easily leave or be replaced

—

Apart from additional leadership and general business acumen, the key skill that professional CEOs bring to the role is a much harder-headed approach to decisions; in particular they're prepared to call time on sacred cows! However, what a hired gun can never match is the passion and bloody-mindedness of a founder. If you can marry the two skills by reinventing yourself as a CEO-founder, then it can be a powerful combination. But of course, get 'founder' off your business card pretty quickly.

This is not intended to antagonise venture capitalists, but I stand by my basic point that most VC investment structures establish an unbalanced relationship with a management team. There are obvious benefits to the entrepreneur as he gets money to spend growing his business, but the trade-off is always significant. Tread carefully!

Opening the Second Office

Mark Terry-Lush
Renegade

PR agency Renegade recently opened its
second office in Bristol and has been quick
to become part of the city's creative scene
thanks in part to award-winning work for the
GCHQ intelligence agency.

There's a scene in Jaws when Roy Schneider sees the size of the shark, staggers backwards and mumbles, "You're gonna need a bigger boat". It's a bit like that the moment you realise that your business needs to expand.

I founded Renegade as a low-risk lifestyle business. I was a freelancer, bringing in other freelancers when I won larger projects that needed to be delivered across Europe. However, as demand for our PR services grew, I started recruiting people full-time in our small office near the Forest of Dean.

After a few successful years, our ambitions evolved to offer new products and services. This was no longer a lifestyle business, we wanted to win new clients in different sectors. But that meant recruiting people with more experience. However, stuck in the middle of (what most people consider) nowhere, it was difficult to attract and retain the right talent.

There were a few options to solve this: 1) offer candidates a lot more money to join us 2) pay for their commute or 3) let them work from home; none of which were ideal. When you're building a small business the last thing you need is fragmentation - and it's not exactly cost effective to increase overheads. Then the penny dropped: we needed a bigger boat, or in our case – an extra one.

Choosing a location was also a challenge. Do we open in a city north or south of our current location? Cheltenham, Birmingham, Bristol or overseas? Despite the majority of our clients being overseas we opened a second office in Bristol, a city with bags of entrepreneurial, friendly, talented people.

There were also additional benefits – access to regional business opportunities and new collaborators. It sounded good and, with its established creative hub, we instantly felt at home. Unfortunately, wanting a second office and making it happen are two very different propositions. It's not that it's difficult, but it is time consuming and costly. There are the practicalities of getting the right space, but you also have to think about how to foster the right environment within it.

As a creative company we wanted something inspiring, relaxed and motivational – so we searched interesting spaces (lofts, studios, etc)

n edgier parts of the city. But, from that grand vision, the process
quickly shifted to the mundane: Are there enough parking spaces?
Who is providing telecoms? Is the broadband quick enough? How
many waste paper bins do we need?

Having an excellent operations manager, who made it his mission to
ind the right location, deal with the logistics, and be accountable for
the opening was a huge benefit. Essential, even.

There were some tricky decisions – such as negotiating the right lease.
We didn't want to be stuck in a five-year contract in case the move
was a flop, but we also needed some security. But actually the most
difficult decisions were conceptual, such as should the new office
be an extension of the existing one or an enterprise in its own right?
As founder, should I head up both offices or would an independent
management structure better suit?

We decided to split the functions, keeping the PR team in
Gloucestershire and building our digital team in Bristol. This would
give the new office its own sense of identity. It made sense on paper,
so we gave the Bristol office its own budget and targets and set it up
to win its own clients. In practice, it took a lot longer than we expected
to pay off. We thought that because we already had contacts, gaining
new business would be easy, but it took a lot longer than we thought
to stand on its own two feet.

If you're thinking of opening a second office, my advice is to set
some expectations and then halve them. It's great to have work in
place from existing clients, but you need somebody hunting out new
business from day one. That's critical. Make sure you set a long-term
strategy detailing how the office will become sustainable and scalable,
and get the right people in place who you trust to deliver it.

After 18 months we've learnt masses and have made several changes;
PR is now a core function of the Bristol office. We're glad we did it
because we've widened our talent pool, won new business, fostered
new relationships and have interesting new collaborators.

We've now opened a satellite office in Berlin, principally to service
our Onitsuka Tiger fashion client. It's literally a couple of desks and a
sneaker showroom in an open-plan creative hub but the lessons learnt
from Bristol have been applied and we have a fantastic person running
the office. So while it's too soon to say we're cruising, we're definitely
better prepared to tackle the big fish.

Managing
International Suppliers

Adam Place
nu desine

If you were to imagine 10 electric drums strapped to a giant robotic head you probably still wouldn't have anything quite as unique as the Alphasphere, Nu Design's groundbreaking instrument which already has orders placed from the US to Japan.

There's a romance behind the idea of international sales, but it's not as easy as it sounds - and flying off to exotic places can quickly become just a long commute.

Recently we've been trying to work out how many countries we've dealt with since prototyping the Alphasphere. Our tool builder is Swedish but based in China, our factories are Chinese, but largely UK-run, and then we have sales reps across America, Japan and Europe. As you can imagine, it all gets a little hectic sometimes.

What we've found is that operating through so many time zones makes business a little slower. We'll send a message raising an issue but our Chinese manufacturers will have already left the office, and by the time they reply we're fast asleep. One thing that's taken a bit of getting used to is waking up to a full inbox. There'll be a barrage of construction emails from Asia and sales emails from the States; and even if you reply right away they won't be received for 12 hours. I had to learn that it was healthier not to check emails unless you were in the office, not just because of the time difference but because of your mindset. Your thought process, list of priorities and tone when just waking up at 7am is very different to somebody who i one foot out of the office at 5pm, and so I had to find that middle ground. I mean, it's tough to be on form for middl of the night Skype meetings!

On the whole it has been a case of slightly altering our working practices, accommodating and compromising with each country's practices along the supply chain. What was important for us was to visit the people who would be involved in our production. Our engineer visited China factories to witness the first plastic moulds being constructed and that probably saved us months of confirming different parts. There tends to be a lot of hysteria about working conditions in China, and all factories are tarred with the same brush, so it was important for us to see the realities and feel comfortable. It was also essential to have that face time with line managers along the supply chain. Just being able to question somebody face-to-face about everything from time lines to recycling; you feel that you are getting more honest information.

his is making it sound like we sailed through an
nternational supply chain with no issues, but of course
hat wasn't the case. As a small company placing our first
rder, we were quite far down the priority list for many
usinesses. It was a scenario that, no doubt, many other
reative companies will have faced: a supplier wanting to
ull back the date while clients want to bring it forward.

s you might expect, the language barrier has thrown up
onfusions from time-to-time. Our Chinese distributors
nce put an advert on 360Buy.com - basically the
hinese Amazon – and wanted the Alphasphere
nmediately, despite us not having built them. They
ouldn't understand why we hadn't delivered the products
ght away, as the concept of demoing prototypes got
ompletely lost in translation. Since that situation we've
een very careful to check that all parties are on the same
age and I think we're all learning from each other.

side from language mishaps we've also had to be very
indful of subtler cultural differences. That isn't just
a seemingly foreign land like China, even in the US
eir sales and business ethos is so different - hunting
r higher margins and being fiercely profit driven. You
eed to understand your partner's attitude to money.
or instance, access to cash in North America is quite

difficult whereas business loans are commonplace in Asia,
and we've noticed that this changes people's attitude to
business negotiations.

We also found that business was more personable in
China; that trust wasn't built and contracts weren't
signed until after a string of compulsory drunken nights.
However, in Japan, where business with the West is more
familiar, contract negotiations were swifter and far more
formal. Of course not everyone is dealing in China, but
these sensitivities are still worth considering even if you
approach a potential collaborator in central London or a
factory in the industrial North.

The main thing we have taken away is to be doubly clear
on what you need from each particular company on the
chain. I don't think we appreciated how good the British
are at unintentionally underplaying issues, and for other
cultures that can cause a gap in expectations. So our
secret was to visit our suppliers, make those connections
and get them enthused about our project so that people
are working with you, not just for you.

How Analytics Can Drive Sales

Mike Hawkyard
4T2

4T2 is an award-winning web agency which specialises in creating online games and fun websites for kids. Recent clients have included CBBC, Lego and Mobil.

I used to think that, of all the jobs in a creative agency, analytics had to be one of the dullest.

It was something for the corporate tech guys, not a games company creating high-octane entertainment where Lego starships blow one another into far-flung galaxies!

But now I'm thinking - what do I know? As technology gets faster and better connected, knowing exactly what your audience gets excited by and what they think sucks, suddenly seems like a pretty smart idea. It's a change which is happening quickly . Only three years ago clients would give us a budget, a time line, and we'd create then launch a game. That was it. Job done. Now, however, we're expected to allocate large parts of the budget, up to 50 per cent, on analysing and adapting a game after it has launched.

Technology has allowed the publishing of creative products to become much more fluid. When games were only released on cassettes or CDs, it was very difficult to get any decent consumer feedback. Of course there were market research sessions, where you could sit down and interview players, or watch them interacting with your game, but it was too subjective. What's more, there was nothing you could do about it, anyway. The game was already out there. With digital publishing we can now mathematically measure how many players use a particular character or on which level most players are turning off, then make changes in real-time to keep future players 'in' the game for longer. These analytics are reinventing industry practice. On the Android platform you can now measure this data in the morning, re-create around it and have a new release for players to download by the afternoon.

While this level of analytics is helping to create some incredible work, as with any new process it takes a while to learn the best way to do it. For instance, there's a real danger in thinking that because something has worked well once, doing it again will be just as successful. So some people will take data from one product - like 'average play time' - and then apply the 'success points' it highlights to all their other work - but it doesn't make any sense. There are just too many variables in creative products to create any meaningful benchmark from it. There's no way the creative is similar enough to mean anything and so you're essentially building from meaningless statistics. While that might sound like pretty game-centric issues, I bet there are directors out there measuring how long one particular film is viewed for compared to their own. Stop it!

One problem with all this analytic potential is that some supposedly creative games are now run by accountants. They'll analyse play data for the most profitable aspects and tell creatives to endlessly recreate it – like a Hollywood production model, I guess! The risk is, does that become too formulaic to be any fun at the end?

If used properly, analytics should make it easier to listen to your audience. We ask our players what they find fun, what they want more or less of and then cater to it. It helps us to create alongside the audience, taking their suggestions and crediting them for it. Personally, I think that's the opposite of formulaic.

Data has to be used, however. Too often agencies will measure a game's success and then use the data to just pat themselves on the back: "Ooh, we had a 72 per cent retention rate; let's go to press!" What they should be doing is measuring why they had that retention rate and using those concepts to plan for another success.

As you might imagine, the use of analytics has gone far beyond the creative-technical process and now trickles down through marketing, sales and business planning. If you can measure which character is the most selected in a game, which character do you think is going to be on our banner ads? It's not just the creatives who need to be on top of the data, it's the sales people and account managers too. Even office managers should probably be looking, if they know that on a Friday 'levels' outsell 'weapons' then whoever manages your staff should be diverting your manpower accordingly.

It's a tricky process and, as with any data, we had to learn which of it actually matters for the business. But whether you're in games, film or advertising - any company which still thinks that analytics is just for the geeks should be looking over their shoulder. The geeks are working out how to blow your business into a far-flung galaxy.

Lola Media helps individuals, companies and brands to understand, creatively develop and monetize new opportunities and business models from the intellectual assets, products and processes they already own, both in the real world and digital space.

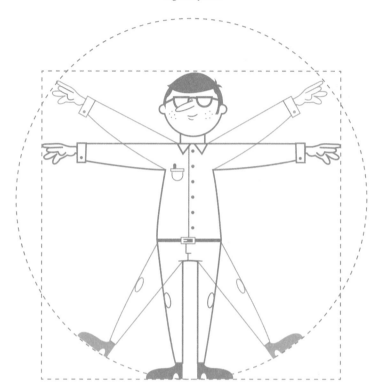

Welcome to the 'creative industries'...

Whether you're fresh out of college, starting full-time work or launching your own business, it's important to ensure you know where you stand with your intellectual property. Now, more than ever before, it is possible to build a 'bank' of your own IP from which you can create different projects on a variety of platforms for your long term personal benefit. But how do you ensure you retain as much IP as possible and are paid fairly for your work? Here are a few suggestions to help you through the minefield...

- Everyone -

| Think of all you create/write/design/ produce as your IP. | View developing your IP as a lifelong investment. | Retain as much ownership of all you create as possible. | Nurture your creations. | Understand what you are selling and learn your rights. |

All your work and related IP is likely to be owned by your employer.

You will have no rights, benefit or ownership in what you produce.

If you produce your own design work privately, ask for a clause giving you ownership to be inserted into your contract.

Working part-time or at a low rate? Try negotiating a share of ownership, revenue/profits of your creativity.

Confirm all IP agreements in an email and ask for confirmation.

- Freelance/Short-Term contract -

Working on an agency's brief? Your freelance contract will generally pass ownership of your work to the client company.

If you're asked to produce work on a tight budget, ask for a clear specification limiting how your work will be used.

Don't start work until you've received a written contract.

Be realistic when negotiating. Know your limit.

- Creative Company/Partnership -

If working for other agencies/clients, ask to be the acknowledged creator.

If you're coming up with a world/character, agree the specified use as it is your copyright.

If you've created something with real potential, offer your clients an exclusive usage license with a set end date, so it will revert to you.

Understand what IP covers – it can be a company asset that can be licensed and sold.

If you are in business with others, set up a contract that covers who owns what IP if you break up.

How to Choose the Right Ideas to Develop

Morgan Francis
Spider Eye

If you haven't heard of Spider Eye then there's a chance your children will have, as having worked on Horrid Henry and Jungle Junction the team are now a staple of Saturday morning TV.

People say that ideas are the life blood of the industry. We all have ideas, but those ideas are only worth something if you can get someone to pay you for them. As Steve Jobs observed: "Real artists ship". The challenge we face every day is trying to decide which ideas our customers are most likely to buy.

In my world, the products are animated shows, but the process of what we choose to develop is probably similar to a lot of other creative mediums – at least that we're all governed by the need to make a profit. Less than one in 200 shows actually make a profit, so we have to try to reduce the odds in favour of ideas which can hit the holy grail of a return on investment.

Often the selection is based on criteria that have little to do with creative merit: is the idea from a freelancer or an existing published book, and if so how much of the IP will we own? Has a show like this been done before? More and more, the determining factor is if it can be merchandised. Does the show contain suitable characters which could become toys? Might a publisher want to create spin-off books from it? Could it be a computer game? However, all of these aspects are ultimately pointless if nobody is looking for your idea.

You need to check market demand. In our case, we review broadcaster commissioning websites to see if our idea is 'what they're looking for at the moment' – is it in vogue? If it's not then it's generally back to the drawing board.

However, when all's said and done we're creatives working in a creative industry and so when that one brilliant idea appears all of these sensible business rules go out the window! That's what we did with Jungle Junction, a hit we created for the Disney Channel. Nobody wanted the show but we believed in it. It may have taken about eight years to sell but now it's broadcast in 150 countries and, yes, the merchandise is selling!

I wouldn't recommend following a gut instinct very often, because it's a major risk to both your finances and your reputation. It comes down to being stubborn I suppose, and fortunately I was in the position of owning an animation company where I could just plough on with my idea. I was going to run with that idea regardless of any advice. It was a case of 'you're all wrong and I'm right!'

After you decide you're going to go for an idea the next stage is to develop a prototype. It's important to remember what you're doing this for. This stage is about determining whether the product will work. In animation, we write a script and develop some character models. This normally gives me a clue as to whether my idea might work but the process will also set you back about eight grand. After that level of commitment, you may be seduced into thinking it's too late to back out at that stage, but you need to be brutal as this is your last chance to scrap an idea before the whole process becomes phenomenally expensive. On the upside, if like me you ploughed on with an idea despite protest then it's normally the point when others might start to go, 'oh, OK maybe he was right.' Sweet vindication!

Once the idea has developed a tangible shape and built some general support, it's probably best to go check with a proper, suited professional customer/commissioner for their reaction. Seeking out the views of your potential clients is a good idea and is something I wouldn't go without. We have found it much better to only ever take our ideas to one client, however, because art is so subjective, 20 potential clients will no doubt give you 20 conflicting opinions. Your head goes in to a spin!

So the process of refining an idea - ensuring it is fit for market, financially viable and, if not, scrapping it - is a long one. Your raw creative weighed against business decisions and while this creates the best chance for your product to succeed I don't know if it necessarily creates the best product. It's a tricky dilemma. The best creative comes when someone sticks to their guns and produces something completely out there. Problem is, 99 per cent of those brilliant ideas will never make it.

It's a decision that you'll have to make early on – do I risk it or create a product designed for market? Despite their being no correct answer, your choice will likely come to define your agency, if not make or break it altogether.

Wrestling With Doubt

Ian Anderson
Overlay Media

The flagship product of mobile data experts Overlay, The Context Engine enables devices to intelligently monitor their own behaviour. This intriguing tech gained them international acclaim in 2012 and led to a successful buy-out bid from Inmobi.

When people say it's lonely at the top, what they really mean is: 'it's hard taking decisions'.

When the buck stops with you, there's nobody else to give your ideas the thumbs up. How are you supposed to know they're right? Maintaining confidence in your own business decisions is a complex issue.

While we need to believe in our company more than anyone else, we also need to realise when our ideas are terrible and try to nip them in the bud. Day to day, I often find myself hammering out conflicting points of view in my brain: will this succeed or won't it? Should I do this – should I do that? Is this a good idea – does it stink? It drives me crazy. These battles underpin a complex dilemma that every business leader has to confront every single day - am I doing the right thing?

Indecision is completely understandable in a changing environment, but it can also be unsettling for investors, customers or employees. Visible indecision may even result in people quickly losing confidence in us. It might be on a much larger scale, but you only have to look at the 2012 US fiscal cliff negotiations to see where uncertainty can lead you. The US Senate's inability to decide on the future budget drove money markets in a spin, press in a lather and incomprehension all round.

The trouble is that decisions never go away, and even once you've make one it's just replaced by another. Take employing a new member of staff - you have to weigh up whether the business can afford the cost; if the business can grow without the increased capacity; or if the finance should instead be invested in new products?

Eventually it becomes ingrained, I guess. I've reached a stage where I'm second guessing decisions all the time in light of what the alternatives might be. Where it gets complicated is when Plan B isn't enough and you start thinking about Plan C too. It can get plain silly, as by the time you're contemplating a Plan D your faith in Plan A has all but evaporated. Not only do your own opinions start conflicting but even your own good ideas!

Do I think too much? Well perhaps, but I was always very keen not to mess up. I found it really frustrating that there was often no way of knowing the answer before it was too late. I wound up treating all significant business decisions as risks that I wanted to avoid or minimise. But I had to learn that business is like life, if you don't take any risks you'll miss out on the experiences that make it all interesting. For a company to live you need t take risks.

All of this worrying about decisions wasn't just causing stress and indecision, it was eating up all of my time. I spent too long considering the views of my advisers and trusted friends. Eventually, I realised I had to listen to myself, I had to start trusting my own judgment. This alone did not address th self-doubt and I had to almost start a mantra in my brain so that I could ease my mind without forever mulling the 'what if's'. For me this strategy was as simple as accepting that at times I would make the wrong decision and that it was okay to do so. While that may sound simplistic it was also liberating.

Even, with all the thinking I dedicated to running my business, not every decision was correct. Nor are they now, but developing that approach to keep the mind at peace was essential in gaining the self-belief necessary to run a business. This stopped me from being my harshest critic and allowed me to focus on the important work, and even occasionally get things right!

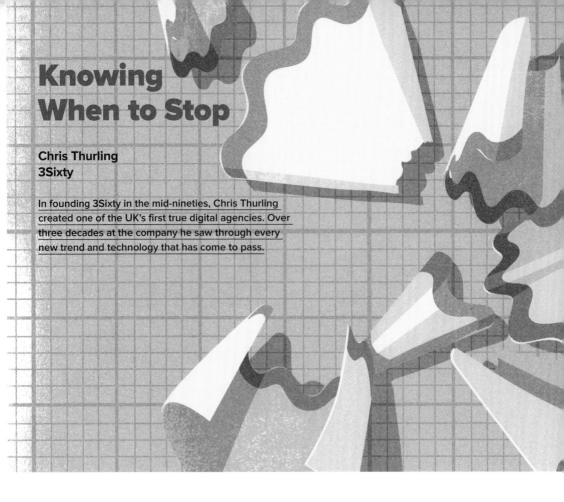

Knowing
When to Stop

Chris Thurling
3Sixty

In founding 3Sixty in the mid-nineties, Chris Thurling
created one of the UK's first true digital agencies. Over
three decades at the company he saw through every
new trend and technology that has come to pass.

In 1993 I was in the politics department at Bristol University when I was shown one of the first ever web browsers, Mosaic. While I was no computer person the idea of it really sparked something in me.

Two years later the web really took off and I saw the
potential for a new type of agency; one that combined
traditional creativity, marketing and design with this
new technology. I guess it's what you'd now call a digital
agency; back then they didn't exist. Instead you had to
start your own, and thankfully I was stubborn-minded
enough to do so. What I wanted to create was an agency
that was recognised for the quality of its work and that
behaved with integrity. I wasn't interested in becoming the
next Bill Gates and money didn't particularly motivate me.

Initially, 3Sixty was a virtual agency - because few people
had those early web skills - and I just project managed
the ones who did. By 2000 the digital market had matured
and we moved the company to an office space in Bristol.

3Sixty began to resemble a regular agency and that's
pretty much the way it stayed until I left in 2012.

The thing about running a creative company is that you
need passion and energy. Very often one drives the other.
I'm 45 now and I was starting to meet clients who were
young enough to be my children! I saw new ideas, and
a new attitude from people who had grown up with the
technology. Looking at the changing faces of the industry
I felt that perhaps I'd reached the peak of what I could
realistically achieve leading a creative digital agency.
After 17 years it was time for me to be involved with the
industry in a slightly different way.

Looking over at the last years at 3Sixty I'll admit the
business didn't turn out exactly the way I'd wanted, but
that's the nature of creative entrepreneurs; you're never
content with your achievements. Better clients, more
enjoyment, more money... there's always something
more! So I was never quite content with 3Sixty, but I can
say I've ever met a company head who was. We're always
itching for the next challenge and that can either be the
fuel to create or it can drive you mad.

The last four years at 3Sixty became increasingly
frustrating for me, as we tried to achieve these high

spirations during an uncertain economic climate. I did
et ground down by that; the fact that the recession
ragged on for so long meant that some of the energy and
ptimism I used to have for the business became hard to
nd. That passion should make you feel like you'd almost
o it for free. If you go in to the creative sector simply
ying to become the next Mark Zuckerberg then you
obably won't succeed. The motives of successful creative
eople are never money but passion for the challenge,
nd so when that is gone you know it's time for a fresh
hallenge. I had made my mind up by summer 2010 and
ld the board that I wanted out within three years.

—

and have a fresh sheet of paper. I had to admit that I'd
fallen out of love with the business and that it was time to
move on. Anyone in that position just has to ask themself if
they have fallen out of love with running a business or with
the actual business itself. The only answer to both of those
questions is not to sit and suffer, otherwise it will grind you
down in to the dust. You'll waste your life and, what with
being in the creative industries, you'll not exactly make a
fortune while doing so. So don't be too proud to move on.

Leaving something you've built is almost like splitting up
with a girlfriend. The anticipation is awful but once you've
actually done it there's an immense sense of liberation; that
you can move on to the next chapter in your life. I'm looking
forward to turning the page.

If you go in to the creative sector simply trying to become the next Mark Zuckerberg then you probably won't succeed

—

may not have been the way I'd envisaged leaving the
usiness but ultimately I've ended up where I wanted

The Delicate Art of Turning Away Clients

Adam Merrifield
White Circle Productions

From their office in Bournemouth, WCP blur the lines between commercial and documentary, with intriguing subjects such as world champion swimmer Fred Bousquet and Portuguese footballer Hulk.

When we started up, every client seemed like gold dust. Our goal was to build a client list, get some cash into the business and keep ourselves alive, so every client seemed important.

Between the financial worries of any start-up and the shaky economy, it was very tempting to accept any work which came our way, no matter how uncreative the work was. Whilst we had some great jobs, we found it all too tempting to take on clients who consumed vast quantities of our time but didn't actually pay us vast quantities of money. We had clients offer fees ten times below our standard rate, but when you're growing it's hard to look beyond any source of cash to get moving.

Once we had been going for a while, we realised that all the time spent servicing clients for small fees could be better spent chasing larger clients with real budgets who wanted really creative work produced. We had taken on too many projects we didn't enjoy, either creatively or financially. It took a few years, but eventually we reached that stage where we felt secure enough to focus on what we wanted White Circle Productions to be.

Ditching any client seemed a brave step. But an important factor we had to consider was that you're only as good as your last job. Working on uncreative projects was generating a bad perception of the business, the quality of the work was low and we weren't proud of it. Most of the time, we wouldn't even promote the fact that we'd worked on a certain project. We just wanted them out of the door. Looking back, it seems obvious that if we weren't confident enough to tell others about our work then why on earth were we producing it?

To help overcome our reservations, we decided to apply a criteria for what constituted a bad client. For us it was clients who consumed time, were uncommunicative, had uncreative projects and/or who negotiated rates too hard early on and weren't getting us anywhere financially. We ran some analysis on how we were reaching our monthly financial target and discovered that, too often, we had been working on 15 smaller, less desirable projects rather than chasing five impressive ones. It wasn't just the quality, it created a lot more work. Working on more individual projects created higher cost of sales – due to more meetings, more changes, more opinions – more hassle. We faced up to these inefficiencies and decided some things had to change.

From then on we began to turn away clients. Some we refused outright and others we stood firm on our costs, so that either they would turn us down or accept it, and we'd have the financial incentive to take on an uncreative project.

For long term clients we began to slowly increase their fees until the point where either they committed to the 'new us' or left us. In all honesty, it was nice to edge out the clients who had negotiated too hard when we were a young company. Everyone wants to feel that they're valued and it's hard to work for clients who aren't prepared to pay you a fair amount – those aren't the people who we are willing to work for anymore.

Nonetheless, there's still a side of you that's apprehensive about not accepting an order or turning away business, especially in this economic climate. On the other hand, you know damn well where it's going to take you. For me it comes down to the fact that I can't run a business on projects I don't respect. It's as simple as that.

Now that we've made this decision to be more selective we have found more time to chase exciting projects with creative interest and a healthy budget. We're the same size company and are still able to generate the same turnover, just more selectively and with clients we can shout about.

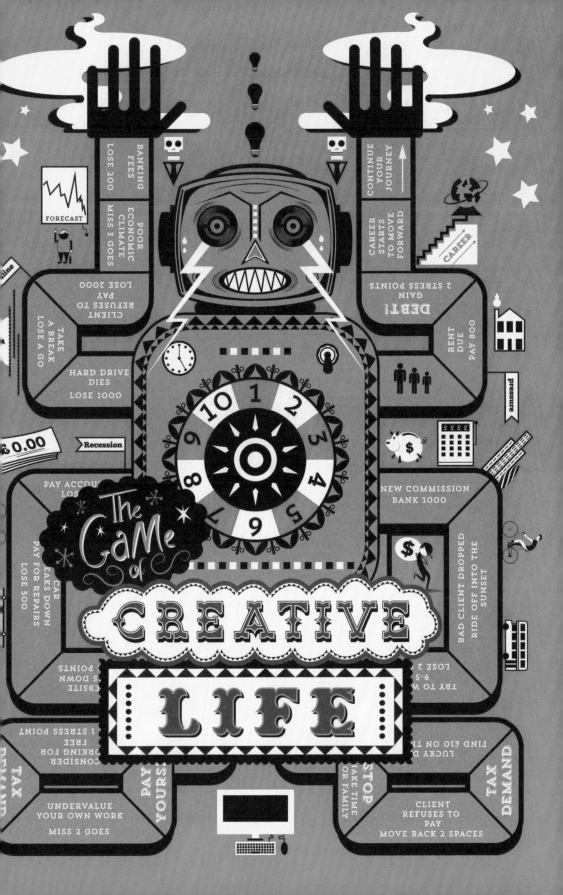

Looking to
the Future

Charles Wace
twofour

Few companies produce content
as varied as Diving with Tom Dailey
and Greatest Plastic Surgery
Shockers, but twofour's range and
breadth has taken it from West
Country start-up to an international
powerhouse with studios in LA and
Abu Dhabi.

Looking to the future?
First off, this is not our latest
clairvoyance show featuring
Derek Acorah; it's the thing that
stops your business becoming
obsolete in five years' time.

It's an essential activity which every business needs to do
no matter their size. The industry moves so fast that, as
the head of a creative company, I need to be a few steps
ahead. To do that I must try and judge what's cresting on
the next wave.

To avoid all the tyre kicking that new possibilities come
with, you first need a pretty clear sense of who you are
as a company. Anyone looking ahead to the next trend or
piece of technology must understand what it is they do
best. That might sound overly simplistic but, in a highly
complicated digital world, it is vital to find your niche
as new tech or trends should only be considered in the
context of how it can help your core offering.

There are really two ways of moving on new trends:
1) Appoint a direct strategy to research and utilise them
or 2) Follow one's hunches. At twofour, I think we have
changed our approach. A few years ago we probably wou
have looked at every exciting new piece of technology ar
given it a try. Now, however, we increasingly look at wha
we do best - in our case, content - and then answer the
question 'how can we make content for a multi-platform
world, and which technology can aid that?'

That's really very different from being a company which
tries doing this and tries doing that, and which tells the
clients that they're 'in to it all'. One of the reasons so
many digital companies go adrift is that they get focuse
on new possibilities and try too many things. Again,
you should be asking if new trends can assist your core
offering and only sign up if the answer is a resolute yes.

Once you have discovered a new 'horizon to follow' ther
still no need to own the whole value chain. In broadcast
second screen viewing is the next big thing, but that
doesn't mean twofour will try and develop second scree
technology. Instead, we will partner with a company whi
has already invested in that market and allow them to
develop the tech while we develop the content. It keeps
you both in your comfort zones also saves you a bucket
load in R&D costs.

at approach should also pervade how and when you
ove on a new technology. Again, using the second
reen example, we all know it will be huge but we
so know that at present it's very hard to profit from.
rsonally I'd rather let a few other trailblazers spend
ousands on pilots and R&D and then we'll be part of the
cond wave when a template is in place. If you slavishly
come a first adopter of new technologies then you're
e one who loses the money while someone else comes
ong and profits afterwards.

—

Nobody quite knows what is going to happen in the near future but that shouldn't stop us trying to find out

—

rtnership is a neat way of avoiding those issues but it
lly depends on what your aspirations are. At twofour
aspire to be Britain's most loved content creation
mpany across multi-platform. We do not aspire to be
chnological trailblazers – and that is probably not what

our clients want from us either. So ask, what do your
clients want?

Nevertheless, media has changed and you will need to keep
an eye on the curve. Only 20 years ago you could produce
a film, everybody would watch it in the cinema and then
clap at the end. Now content has to be made to deliver in
lots of different directions, you really have to sweat your
product and there's much less clapping at the end. But the
proliferation of new platforms means that all media is now
widely consumed. That opportunity should excite creatives
because for the first time ever start-ups can now reach
the same audience as the establishment! The trick really
comes full circle to my first point; if you are a new agency,
figure out what it is you do best and then research which
platforms or new technologies will assist you.

Nobody quite knows what is going to happen in the near
future but that shouldn't stop us trying to find out.

Creative Index

Aaron Miller

www.aaronmillerillustration.com

Adam Koehli

www.adamkoehli.co.uk

Ben Steers

www.bensteers.com

Blue & the Bughou

by Bertie Telezynski & Rachel Le

Gav Strange

www.jam-factory.com

Hello

www.01134.co.uk

I See Heroes

www.iseeheroes.com

Jake Applebee

www. crackmagazine.ne

Lesley Nichols

www.lesleynichols.com

Little Whale Studio

www.littlewhalestudio.com

Naomi Dodds

www.naomidodds.com

Nick Raven

www.nick-raven.co.uk

his book has been compiled alongside over 30 of
e South West's most exciting artists and designers.
ease take the time to visit their sites, view more of
eir work and where possible support their talents.
e promise you won't be disappointed.

hris Malbon
w.chrismalbon.co.uk

Digitally Roasted
www.digitallyroasted.co.uk

Fiasco Design
www.fiascodesign.co.uk

Flytopia
by Karni & Saul

ke Ivill
w.jakeivill.co.uk

Jamie Jones
www.whoisjamiejones.com

John Owens
www.eskimocreative.com

Jordan Carter
www.jordanandrewcarter.co.uk

Iiver Sin
w.oliversin.com

Pixillion
www.pixillion.com

Rebecca Cleal
www.whiteduckscreenprint.co.uk

Rebecca Kaye
www.rebeccajkaye.com

Ross Cleaver

www.rossiscleaver.com

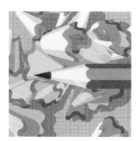

Slumber Bean

www.slumberbean.com

Slumber Bean

www.slumberbean.com

Sneaky Raccoon

www.sneakyraccoon.com

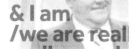

Studio Ade

www.designbystudioade.com

Taxi Studio

www.taxistudio.co.uk

Thought Den

www.thoughtden.co.uk

Tom Lane

www.gingermonkeydesign.co

Tom Lane

www.gingermonkeydesign.com

Tom Redfern

www.iamtom.net

Tom Sydenham

www.antlaclad.com

Vector Meldrew

www.vectormeldrew.com

Creative England

Creative England is a national agency that invests in and supports creative ideas, talent and businesses in film, TV, games and digital media. It aims to grow the brightest, the best, and those with the most promise so that individuals and businesses can achieve their full creative and commercial potential.

For more information, visit www.creativeengland.co.uk.

The iNet

The Creative Industries iNet (Innovation Network) is a £3.2 million programme of support designed to help the South West's creative businesses thrive and advance the area's growing reputation as a global creative centre of excellence. The iNet is funded by the European Regional Development Fund and led by Creative England.

For more information, visit www.creativeindustriesi.net

Anthony Story

Anthony specialises in developing and delivering new strategies for change, growth and results. He runs the Creative iNet for Creative England, a £3.2m innovation programme directly supporting the growth strategies of over 300 creative businesses.

He ran an award-winning, consumer engagement and communications agency for seven years, delivering target-driven business and social campaigns. These covered cross-platform concept, brand, content and marketing production - across web, mobile, video, design, games, events and print, usually at the same time.

He has produced and edited many websites; written two documentaries, two plays, a virtual museum and a thousand articles and case studies. He started out as a director and producer and also starred in Portugal's biggest grossing domestic film – a good way to discover acting wasn't his strong point.

Daniel Humphry

Daniel has been freelance writing and editing for national press in the UK and Australia since graduating in 2007. On any given day he can be found editing business pieces for serious publications while moonlighting articles about spandex clad men, defensive midfielders or cartoon villains for wrestling, football and animation titles alike.

He is also the founder of OFF LIFE - a street press comic aimed at getting more people reading smart, adult comics. One day he wants to make a cartoon.

Notes

★ To ensure people feel involved in your company, you need to invest in community ~~capacity~~ building = meeting your customers @ events as much as possible. Get their help. Still lots of radio + PR.

★ Full - service/multi service = bespoke/tailored response.

★ Selling Time vs Selling products
- Work 4 Hire is low risk but low reward.
- profits _{margins} will always be limited (20-30 %. max).
- few ppl want 2 invest in a work 4 hire business model.
+ once a ~~company~~ Company produces a successful product, pleg g IP, companys will come Knocking!

★ 4 key elements 4 a brand with integrity
   ① Coherence
   ② Consistency
   ③ Legibility
   ④ mystery.

who are we, what r we going 2 offer, what are our struggles? ← that's ur brand!
• work with clients who match your style.
• "pay peanuts, get monkeys"
• take your ego out of the project